"With practical, accessible, neurodiversity-affirming skills for neurodivergent p within a prescriptive nonfiction industry that so often overlooks us."

—**Devon Price**, author of *Unmasking Autism*

"This is the right book at the right time. Both Jennifer and Monique have a deep understanding of the challenges that neurodivergent people face in our community, but also a broad knowledge of strategies that work to cope with the challenges. I can highly recommend this book to assist neurodivergent people to thrive, but also to all those who live, love, and work with them."

—**Michelle Garnett, PhD, Psych**, clinical psychologist; and founder and director of Attwood & Garnett
Events, AuDHD

"Like a warm hug and as if entering a dimly lit, quiet room after hours of overstimulation, this book is a heart-warming sigh of relief. As a neurodivergent person, I found myself crying of joy and gratitude for being seen so deeply while reading it. Like a kind friend or the sweetest pet, this book can serve as a loving companion to all who read it."

—**Janina Scarlet, PhD**, author of *Superhero Therapy*

"This book will make you work, it will make you think, and at times it might even make you cry—but mostly it will make you wish you had read it a decade ago. A great gift for all the neurodivergent people you care about (and especially for yourself)."

—**Sandra Thom-Jones, PhD**, honorary professor at University of Wollongong,
principal of www.autisticprofessor.com, and author of *Growing into Autism*

"This book provides clear, compassionate, and practical advice for anyone wanting to understand, accommodate, and embrace their neurodivergence. I've met so many people who have been given a diagnosis, but no real support to work out what their needs are or how they can improve their mental health. This book fills that gap, a must-read for anyone newly diagnosed."

—**Alice Nicholls**, **DClinPsy**, Autistic clinical psychologist specializing in Autistic burnout,
and creator of the Autistic Burnout Recovery Programme

"Unputdownable. I started reading this and kept going, and I bet you will too. A well-paced read for anyone who wants to understand neurodivergence in adults. This book is a science-backed way for ADHDers and Autistic people to build their strengths, manage their challenges and, above all, accept themselves. Packed with information and practical strategies."

—**Louise L. Hayes, PhD**, clinical psychologist; founder of DNA-V; and coauthor of *What Makes You
Stronger, Get Out of Your Mind and into Your Life for Teens, Your Life Your Way*, and *The Thriving Adolescent*

"Discovering you're neurodivergent as an adult can often bring more questions than answers. Unfortunately, invalidation, misinformation, and unhelpful responses from your nearest and dearest are all too common. Jennifer and Monique—both late-identified neurodivergent themselves—throughout *The Neurodivergence Skills Workbook for Autism and ADHD* offer you much-needed compassion, companionship, clarity, guidance, and skills to navigate this process of better understanding and supporting your unique and beautiful neurodivergent self."

—**Aisling Leonard-Curtin, MSc**, ADHDer; senior psychologist at ADHD Ireland; codirector of Act
Now Purposeful Living; and coauthor of the number one bestseller, *The Power of Small*

The Social Justice Handbook Series

As culture evolves, we need new tools to help us cope and interact with our social world in ways that feel authentic and empowered. That's why New Harbinger created the *Social Justice Handbook* series—a series that teaches readers how to use practical, psychology-based tools to challenge and transform dominant culture, both in their daily lives and in their communities.

Written by thought leaders in the fields of psychology, sociology, gender, and ethnic studies, the *Social Justice Handbook* series offers evidence-based strategies for coping with a broad range of social inequities that impact quality of life. As research has shown us, social oppression can lead to mental health issues such as depression, anxiety, trauma, lowered self-esteem, and self-harm. These handbooks provide accessible social analysis as well as thoughtful activities and exercises based on the latest psychological methods to help readers unlearn internalized negative messages, resist social inequities, transform their communities, and challenge dominant culture to be equitable for all.

The handbooks also serve as a hands-on resource for therapists who wish to integrate an understanding and acknowledgment of how multiple social issues impact their clients to provide relevant and supportive care.

For a complete list of books in
the *Social Justice Handbook* series,
visit newharbinger.com

The Neurodivergence Skills Workbook for Autism and ADHD

Cultivate Self-Compassion,
Live Authentically, and
Be Your Own Advocate

Jennifer Kemp, MPsych
Monique Mitchelson, MPsych

New Harbinger Publications, Inc.

Publisher's Note

NEW HARBINGER PUBLICATIONS is a registered trademark of New Harbinger Publications, Inc.

New Harbinger Publications is an employee-owned company.

Copyright © 2024 by Jennifer Kemp and Monique Mitchelson
New Harbinger Publications, Inc.
5720 Shattuck Avenue
Oakland, CA 94609
www.newharbinger.com

Cover design by Sara Christian

Acquired by Tesilya Hanauer

Edited by Jody Bower

Printed in the United States of America

26   25   24

10   9   8   7   6   5   4   3

To *person 0* and *person 1*—this is for you.
(I love you.)

—Jennifer

To the wonderful neurodivergent community and our allies, and to everyone
who brings compassion and kindness to the world.

—Monique

Contents

Foreword

As a multiply neurodivergent individual, it is my great pleasure to endorse this book and reassure the Autistic and ADHD community that this is a helpful tool for our toolkit that is actually affirming of our neurodivergence.

When Jennifer and Monique asked me to write the foreword for their new book, I was honored because it meant they valued my voice and my lived experience—something we neurodivergent people aren't used to!

Not only that, but I was also impressed they asked me because I'm proudly pedantic. If anyone follows me on social media, you'll know I have somewhat high standards when it comes to anything neurodiversity-affirming—and for a very good reason too.

I was diagnosed with Autism and ADHD when I was a child, over 20 years ago, which meant I grew up in the deficit era of Autism. I grew up hearing narratives that I was broken, that I was too much, that I was a burden, that there was something wrong with me, and that I needed to be fixed. And let me tell you, this shaped my childhood, my teen years, and my twenties from depression to anxiety to self-hate to believing I shouldn't exist.

I believed this until six years ago…when I discovered the concept of neurodiversity and was offered a new narrative. Since then, I've been providing resources, talks, and workshops on neurodiversity and neurodivergence, and I've been critical of the pathology paradigm and the disorder label for even longer. I guess you could say I'm passionate about making sure no one else grows up hating themself or viewing themself as less than for being Autistic or an ADHDer.

I'm someone who understands how important it is to be surrounded by a narrative that affirms our differences, and this workbook does just that. I think, even more significantly, it affirms our differences and needs *without* dismissing our very real challenges and difficulties. So, if I say this workbook is neurodiversity-affirming and doesn't try to fix or change our Autism or ADHD, I genuinely mean it.

As an example of how affirming this workbook is, Monique and Jennifer share tools and strategies for supporting our challenges with executive functioning without labeling them as deficits. See, I don't believe we have executive functioning deficits but instead, we have executive functioning *differences*. If neurotypical people aren't the benchmark for what is normal, how on earth can we have deficits?

That's not to say we can't find our executive functioning differences disabling or distressing but, too often, resources and books will focus on improving our executive functioning skills instead of finding ways to work with our differences. Not this one, though.

I think, most importantly, this workbook is an opportunity for Autistic people and ADHDers to explore and honor their needs and challenges without having their needs or challenges framed as a burden or deficit. I can't begin to express how empowering that is.

When you go through this workbook, you'll discover strategies and tools to support your Autism and ADHD, but what's extra cool is how this workbook acknowledges the unfair, neuronormative ideals and expectations that are reinforced throughout society—and how this plays a part in our journey of self-acceptance and supporting our neurodivergence. I genuinely believe a significant part of looking after our wellbeing is challenging neuronormativity and reframing the expectations and ideals that we measure ourselves against. And this workbook provides many opportunities for us to do so.

This is what sets it apart from other workbooks for us Autistic people and ADHDers. It recognizes that we do not exist in a vacuum and that cultivating a life of acceptance means acknowledging the very real impact of living in a world that disadvantages and oppresses us. I believe this workbook will allow Autistic people and ADHDers to connect with their authentic selves and create a meaningful life in which we can thrive instead of always just surviving.

You'll probably want to dive into this workbook now, so I'll just leave you with this: this isn't about finding a light at the end of the tunnel because, honestly, the tunnel never ends, but it is about illuminating the tunnel with self-acceptance, helpful tools, and a supportive community.

And on behalf of an Autistic ADHDer and a multiply neurodivergent person, thank you Monique and Jennifer for your lived experience–informed workbook. I know it'll be a wonderful resource for Autistic people and ADHDers around the world.

May you continue to be your authentic self in the face of neuronormativity.

—Sonny Jane Wise

Your Journey to Self-Compassion and Self-Acceptance Starts Here

Truth is so rare, it is delightful to tell it.

—Emily Dickinson

Your unique perspective on the world sets you apart from others in ways that can sometimes feel painful. People tell you to "try harder," "focus more," "not take things so personally," or "sort yourself out," but what you do never seems to be quite right. Feeling the weight of other people's disappointment, you work hard to avoid making mistakes. Over time, other people's criticism becomes how you speak to yourself. When you are worried that people might reject you for being weird or rude, it can feel safer to pretend to be someone you are not and try to keep everyone happy. In the process, you lose sight of who you are.

These are just some of the challenges you can face as a neurodivergent person who has different skills, preferences, sensitivities, abilities, and needs (Dwyer 2022). *Neurodivergence* is an umbrella term that includes Autism, attention deficit hyperactivity disorder (ADHD), dyspraxia, dyslexia, dyscalculia, obsessive-compulsive disorder (OCD), Tourette syndrome, tic disorder, bipolar disorder, schizophrenia, and more. This book focuses on Autism and ADHD because these types of neurodivergence, or *neurotypes,* are closely related and share many of the same features and challenges. Whether you have a formal diagnosis or self-identify as Autistic or an ADHDer, this book offers a pathway to understanding yourself better and building a life on a foundation of self-acceptance and self-compassion. If you are someone who has a different neurotype or diagnosis, or differs in some other way from what society views as "normal," aspects of this book will be helpful for you, too.

The later in life you learn you are neurodivergent, the more complicated and challenging your life may have become. The aim of this book is to help you approach yourself with greater kindness and compassion. You will learn the core skills needed to navigate the world as a neurodivergent person, using these skills to create an authentic, meaningful, and satisfying life that works better for you. To develop these skills, we've explored what the research reveals about what it means to be Autistic or an ADHDer, weaving what we learned with our life experiences and those of our clients and friends. We are thrilled to have you on this journey with us.

Uncovering Our Hidden Neurodivergence

As members of the neurodivergent-affirming community, we learn more every day about what it means to be neurodivergent. We have joined the growing number of health professionals who are developing a deeper understanding of this. Throughout this book we use identity-first language and capitalize Autism and Autistic to reflect how proud we are of our neurodivergent identities. (You'll learn more about identity-affirming language in the next chapter.)

Jennifer's Story

I only found out that I was Autistic at forty-seven years old, when one of my children was assessed and I sat in on the interview. As we stepped through each phase of the assessment process, my funny, quick-witted, and observant teenager kept looking over at me, saying, "No, I don't do that—but my mother does." Despite having suspected for some time that my slightly chaotic teen was Autistic, it had never occurred to me that I could be, too.

You might think that as a clinical psychologist, I would have known all about Autism and could recognize it in myself, but this wasn't the case. I'd learned virtually nothing about Autism at university and had only a basic, deficit-focused understanding of how it presents in children. Now it was as if I was Alice in Wonderland and had just stepped through the looking glass—everything suddenly seemed unfamiliar, yet the same. For several weeks, I became lost in my thoughts and overwhelmed with a sense of loss and confusion. Yet very quickly, my life experiences started to make sense in a new way.

At first, I kept my discoveries to myself, because even though I had been working on being kinder to myself for a long time, I still blamed myself for the problems I'd experienced. As a recovering perfectionist, making mistakes tends to make me feel sick to my stomach, yet here I was, going over every awkward social interaction I'd ever had, how I'd lost friends over the years, how I blamed myself for misunderstanding the situation or saying the wrong thing. It was excruciating. Since then, I've continued to reevaluate my life, but at a slower, gentler pace. I still have decades of lived experiences to unpack.

I'd never appreciated how socially awkward I could be, because I grew up in an environment where my differences were accepted. I can lovingly describe my extended family as a bunch of warm and caring geeks with a wide selection of deep interests. I never felt odd or unusual in that environment; little quirks were normal to us. Furthermore, I performed well academically. I thrived on structure, particularly when I created a routine. In my final years of high school, strict dieting and an emerging eating disorder gave me a sense of control at a time when I had some devastating friendship breakdowns.

At the end of high school, a guidance counselor told me my skills would be a good fit for engineering or architecture, but I chose to study psychology anyway. This was the official start of my lifelong passion for learning about humans. I had a shaky start but made good friends with others who shared my interests in my second year. We are all still working in psychology. Most of my closest friends are psychologists, have studied psychology, or work in related fields.

I have been incredibly privileged to pursue a career in my area of passion. While my personal journey toward self-compassion may have started with letting go of my perfectionistic self-criticism, having the opportunity to reevaluate everything has given me a much deeper sense of appreciation and warmth toward myself. Being Autistic has caused me problems, but it has also given me an endless fascination with my work; I never run out of things to learn. It has also given me skills in pattern recognition and analysis, plus the drive to understand things more deeply, all of which I've brought to my writing. As a result, I've been able to unmask more, ask for what I need, and be more authentically myself. I hope to help you do this too.

Monique's Story

Finding my unique neurodivergent identity and getting a diagnosis helped me understand and put into context many things about myself. My whole life, I had been searching for a way to understand why I thought differently and related differently to others. I first suspected I was Autistic when I attended a training session on Autism in adults and women by Tony Attwood, a noted British expert on Autism. I was a psychologist working in a private practice that specialized in Autism and ADHD in Brisbane, yet most of my training was child-focused, while I worked only with adults. During the session, I resonated with many facets of what Autism looks like outside of gender norms. I recognized that many of my struggles and strengths lie in being Autistic. At the time, there were few resources or supports for adult women, and much of the information was negative or deficit-based. I didn't know where to go from there, so I stopped looking into it.

Fast forward a few years. As the neurodiversity-affirming movement gained ground, I was introduced to more empowering information about Autism and ADHD. Understanding why I needed so much recovery time from social events and why I had difficulty navigating social cues helped me unravel the perfectionism and self-criticism I had developed early on in life. Having a logical explanation of the why helped to release any self-criticism I had over being anxious about making social mistakes, managing new situations, feeling sick and dizzy in shopping centers, or having quirky interests and deep obsessions. It also helped me understand why I burn out more quickly than others. I found that the more I learned about Autism and ADHD, the more compassion I developed for myself and others. I was able to understand why others thought differently and acted in ways that did not make sense to me. I could make more space for rest and engage in my interests deeply without apology.

Gradually, I have developed radical self-acceptance for myself and my needs and tailored my life to suit my neurodivergence. I have been able to work in a career that I love and am very passionate about. I can pursue my interests through my work and find flexible work where I am not punished because I need to work part-time and need specific accommodations. I have been able to avoid a generational family pattern of burning out and being unable to participate in the workplace despite having so much to give to society. I am grateful to have supportive colleagues and a boss, friends, and family who have been willing to learn about neurodivergence—many of whom are also neurodivergent! I have found that connecting with other neurodivergent people has been critical on my path to self-acceptance and self-validation. In particular, connecting with fellow neurodivergent mental health professionals and feeling part of a community has been so helpful. I also love working with my neurodivergent clients!

By capitalizing on my unique neurodivergent strengths, I have carved out a life that works for me. I have an excellent memory for facts related to my interests and intense interest and curiosity for learning and accumulating knowledge in various areas, including psychology, social justice, animals, spirituality and religions, yoga, nutrition, and medicine. I analyze data, see patterns and systems, and communicate clearly and directly by cutting through the bullshit. I save energy and manage burnout better by getting support and accommodations where needed and dropping unhelpful expectations of myself. I now live with some chronic health conditions that make life more challenging. My self-compassion skills have been helpful in navigating these difficulties with authenticity.

The Unique Focus of This Book

Autism and ADHD are neurodevelopmental conditions that are common in our society, with approximately 5 percent of the population meeting the criteria for ADHD (Sciberras et al. 2022) and at least 2.8 percent meeting the criteria for Autism (Maenner et al. 2023), although these rates may be higher. Autism and ADHD are genetic, with recent research finding ADHD to be approximately 74 percent inherited (Faraone and Larsson 2019) and Autism to be approximately 90 percent inherited (Sandin et al. 2017). This explains why you will often find ADHD and Autism in multiple generations of the same family.

Interestingly, Autism and ADHD share the same genetic origins. Many people meet the criteria for both Autism and ADHD; recent research indicates that approximately 86 percent of Autistic people could also meet the criteria for ADHD and approximately 50 percent of ADHDers could be diagnosed with Autism (Knott et al. 2021; Rommelse et al. 2010), although these figures may underestimate the overlap. Many of the daily challenges described by ADHDers are also reflected in the difficulties experienced by Autistic people, including sensory differences (Kamath et al. 2020) and repetitive behaviors (La Buissonnière-Ariza et al. 2021). Given this, Autism and ADHD may be better understood as part of a shared spectrum of neurobiological differences that originate from differences in the structure and function of the brain and spinal cord (central nervous system), peripheral nervous system, and other physiological systems (Askham 2020; Barnea-Goraly et al. 2014; Careaga, Van de Water, and Ashwood 2010). The genes responsible for Autism and ADHD can be found in every cell of your body and may be related to differences and difficulties in any part of your body, including digestion, sensory perception, muscle function, pain, heart rate, blood pressure, and hormones.

This book explores the overlapping challenges experienced by Autistic people and ADHDers, including neurodivergent burnout, managing difficult emotions, becoming overburdened by competing demands, feeling extremely hurt by rejection, and trying to hide these differences to avoid negative judgments. Each chapter will guide you toward a more rewarding and fulfilling life as a proud neurodivergent person, whether you have been formally diagnosed or self-identify as Autistic, an ADHDer, or both. Where an issue relates specifically to ADHD or to Autism, we will highlight this; however, for the most part, we will leave it for you to decide whether a particular topic applies to you. If you belong to any other neurominority or are a partner, family member, ally, carer, or health professional working with neurodivergent people, there will be something useful for you in these pages too.

The Opportunity for Self-Compassion

As a neurodivergent person, you are more likely to be criticized, corrected, and judged negatively and feel greater shame and lower self-worth as a result (Price 2022). Autistic people and ADHDers tend to be harder on themselves than their non-neurodivergent peers and have lower levels of self-compassion (Cai et al. 2023; Galvin et al. 2021; Willoughby and Evans 2019). Being self-critical can become so familiar that it feels easier to be harsh and critical toward yourself than to offer yourself kindness and understanding.

Being compassionate means having sensitivity to suffering in yourself and others, with a commitment to try to alleviate and prevent this suffering (Steindl 2020; Gilbert 2009). *Self-compassion* is an active process of approaching yourself with empathy, nonjudgment, and understanding. Higher levels of self-compassion can improve your psychological wellbeing and quality of life while helping you to regulate your emotions, lower your anxiety and stress, and improve your mood (Beaton, Sirois, and Milne 2022; Farmer et al. 2023; Gilbert 2009; Kirby, Tellegen, and Steindl 2017; Wilson et al. 2023).

To help you develop self-compassion skills, we will be drawing on techniques from compassion-focused therapy (CFT). CFT is an innovative approach to therapy that can help you learn how to offer yourself greater compassion. Much more than just having warm feelings toward yourself, self-compassion can support radical and profound positive change in your life—starting with simply pausing to notice what you need and deciding to try to meet these needs. If you tend to be hard on yourself, you may believe that your chances of becoming more self-compassionate are slim, but let us assure you that learning to approach yourself with greater self-compassion is possible.

To help you build these skills, we will integrate CFT approaches with acceptance and commitment therapy (ACT), adapting both to meet neurodivergent needs. Pronounced as one word, ACT, this simple yet powerful approach to therapy offers enormous potential to help neurodivergent people. Rather than treating surface-level symptoms or trying to change the content of your thoughts, ACT focuses on learning to accept yourself and building your ability to navigate difficult and uncomfortable experiences. By developing your skills of present-moment awareness, ACT can help you develop a sense of perspective, tune in to your internal experiences as they happen, and take steps toward what is important to you, even in the presence of self-criticism and doubt. Put together, CFT and ACT can help you create a fulfilling and rewarding life.

How to Read This Book

How you work through this book will be unique to you. We have a few suggestions that may help even when you have less energy, ability to focus, or time.

Complete the first three chapters before moving on. Chapters 1 and 2 are the foundation of the book; you'll learn the fundamentals of the Autistic and ADHD neurotypes, explore your unique expression of neurodivergence, and understand the challenges you face in day-to-day life. This is an essential starting point for developing greater self-compassion and self-acceptance. Chapter 3 focuses on neurodivergent burnout, something that almost all our Autistic and ADHDer clients struggle with—and we suspect you may too. When you are in burnout, you have fewer internal resources available to make positive changes in your life, so learning how to alleviate and prevent burnout is essential for your immediate and long-term wellbeing. Putting these strategies into action right away will also help you complete the rest of the book.

Lean on your strengths to make learning easier. Our aim is to make this book as accessible as possible for neurodivergent thinkers. To achieve this, we blend detailed information with checklists, self-reflection exercises, and practical strategies that you can use immediately. We encourage you to complete the activities using any approach that matches your learning style and personal strengths. You may like to respond to questions by writing in the space provided, using bullet points, creating a mind map, or drawing a comic or animation. You may prefer to record your responses using audio or video. Make this book your own by writing or drawing your responses anywhere you like on the pages (you have our permission to be messy), or use a separate notebook, sketchbook, or folder.

We also understand that sitting still to complete mindfulness activities can be tricky for many people—we have had this experience ourselves. So, feel free to move your body any way you choose during these activities: stand, walk, swing, sway gently from side to side, use a fidget toy, draw, color in, knit, or paint.

Many neurodivergent people have difficulty with visualization. This is called *aphantasia* and is a normal part of human diversity. If this applies to you, you may prefer to draw your responses, search for images that reflect the topic, or write down your thoughts and read these aloud. In other words, work through this book in whatever way suits you best.

Approach this book as if you plan to reread it. As much as you can, try to let go of needing to complete every activity perfectly, as this will slow your progress. From personal experience, we know this can be hard to do. There is no prize for reading this book "properly." Each time you read this book you will gain new insights, so planning to reread it will help you avoid getting stuck. Even though we hope you can attempt each activity, skipping to the next task is okay if you get bogged down or feel overwhelmed. Use a sticky note or write a brief message in the margin to highlight what you want to return to, then move on.

Consider finding a partner for your journey. It is often easier to get things done if you have someone with you. Finding a fellow traveler for this journey could make it easier for you. You may like to invite a friend or partner to read the book with you, complete the activities together or separately, and discuss what you learn. Alternatively, you could take turns reading a section and summarizing it for each other. If you know other people who would like to work through this book, you could create a small online group—your own neurodivergent book club.

Prepare to feel uncomfortable at times. As you work through this book, you may discover new things about yourself or come in contact with painful memories of the past. Treat yourself with extra care and kindness in these moments, and remember to seek the help of an affirming health professional if you feel too distressed. In fact, you may like to work through this book with the help of your therapist.

Work at your own pace. We cover a lot of ground in this book. If you feel intimidated or overburdened at any stage, lower the expectations you have of yourself. Consider setting yourself the goal of reading just a few pages every day or each week. It is better not to change everything at once, so consider aiming for just one small action each day to improve your life.

Be patient with your progress. This book will help you design and build an authentic and purposeful life. However, it will take time. There are many skills to learn along the way. While you are likely to make some quick gains initially, the compounded effect of many small changes will only become more evident over weeks, months, and years. Keep this long-term perspective in mind as you make daily choices to care for yourself. Things will get better with gentle persistence and time.

It is now time to begin. We can't wait.

CHAPTER 1

Getting to Know Yourself in a New Way

If you're lucky enough to be different, never change.

—Taylor Swift

Your neurodivergence is not a superpower—it's much more complicated than that. Whether Autistic or an ADHDer, you experience and interpret the world differently. While being neurodivergent may come with some noticeable benefits, these are balanced with extra challenges (Artemisia 2018), leading to a *spiky profile* of strengths and difficulties. None of us can be brilliant at everything, but because you live in a society that rarely accommodates these difficulties, you are likely to experience greater obstacles in everyday life.

Traditionally, assessing and diagnosing neurodivergence has involved comparing a person's observable behaviors and "deficits" to a list of characteristics defined in the *Diagnostic and Statistical Manual of Mental Disorders*, 5th edition text revision (DSM-5-TR) (American Psychiatric Association 2022) and the International Classification of Diseases and Related Health Problems, 11th revision (ICD-11; World Health Organization 2019). You are considered to meet the diagnostic criteria if you demonstrate enough of the listed behaviors.

This approach has many weaknesses. Early definitions of Autism and ADHD emerged from studies that measured the "disturbances of affective contact" of boys (Kanner 1943). Unfortunately, modern diagnostic criteria are still primarily built on the experiences of white boys and men. Most assessments are based on a limited set of observable behaviors without considering other potential expressions of Autism and ADHD that can emerge from the same neurobiological origins. Those who hide or internalize their neurodivergent differences and show fewer obvious behavioral patterns are routinely overlooked, particularly in women, trans and nonbinary folk; those from First Nations; and people of color (Henderson, Wayland, and White 2023). Many are denied diagnosis because they have developed coping strategies that hide the behaviors listed in these criteria, yet have subtle behavior patterns and an inner experience consistent with neurodivergence.

When I was a child, my mother spent a lot of time teaching me to "behave properly." She expected me to hold eye contact in every social situation, speak up about my needs, and put up with long, boring family parties without complaining. She even tried to teach me how to walk with my arms swinging, saying that walking with my arms by my side was too "odd." I tried to explain that loud noises hurt my head and that being around lots of people exhausted me. I began to slip away from family events as soon as no one was watching. No one ever considered that I was Autistic—it wasn't something girls had back then. I've had a lot of anxiety over my life and wonder whether things would have been different if my Autism had been noticed as a child. —Alice

Fortunately, skilled clinicians are starting to recognize that the differences in how Autistic people and ADHDers experience the world may not always be easily observable (Henderson, Wayland, and White 2023). We can now identify six information processing differences that directly influence your experience of life as a neurodivergent person:

1. Orienting your life around your interests

2. Executive functioning that is often overloaded

3. Experiencing the world and yourself differently through your senses

4. Having difficulty understanding and regulating your emotions

5. Approaching social situations with expectations of equity, fairness, and consistency

6. Communicating directly, accurately, and in detail

In this chapter, you will explore these differences and the challenges you might experience as a result. Depending on your unique expression of neurodivergence, some parts may apply to you more than others, so look for the points that resonate most. It could be helpful to highlight anything that closely reflects your experience as you work through each section.

Orienting Your Life Around Your Interests

A defining feature of neurodivergence is that our lives tend to revolve around our interests. Whether you are Autistic or an ADHDer, you are likely to either feel an intense interest in something or no interest at all. Things that are not interesting for you will barely keep your attention, while other interests can become long-term fascinations and may even define your career.

Pursuing Lifelong Fascinations in Autism

All humans have a limited amount of attention that must be distributed between many competing demands. *Monotropism* is a theory of attention developed by Dinah Murray that describes how Autistic people tend to have a narrow and deep focus of attention. Autistic people's lives are often centered on their interests, which are explored in great depth and for a long time—sometimes a lifetime. Interests can be specific and narrow, such as being fascinated by a sub-branch of physics, or more conceptual, such as being interested in unusual words, phrases, grammar, and linguistics. By comparison, non-neurodivergent people often hold many different interests and have varying degrees of attraction to each. They may have a less detailed understanding of these topics (a *polytropic* approach) and be more focused on social communication (Murray, Lesser, and Lawson 2005).

Monotropism can explain a great deal of the Autistic experience. Strongly pulling your attention, your monotropic interests can engage you in ways that other things cannot. You may spend a great deal of time involved in your interests at the expense of other learning, and overlook essential yet tedious tasks unrelated to your passions, including learning other people's social rules. When you don't spend time on things regularly, you have fewer opportunities to fully develop those skills (Murray, Lesser, and Lawson 2005).

Autistic people have reclaimed the somewhat patronizing term "special interests" to call these long-term fascinations *spins*. When you are focused on your monotropic interest, you are said to be *in your spin*. Spins can be topics or niche interests that do not align with the expectations of everyday life, but which offer you joy. Others may judge your spins as "not a productive use of your time," but this is not the point of a spin. Collecting, researching, documenting, cataloging, and organizing information or items that form part of your spins is inherently satisfying.

When engaged in your spin, you may be less concerned about social conventions and may become so engrossed in talking about your spin that you miss the subtle signs that others are not as interested in the topic as you. When fully engrossed in a monotropic tunnel, it can feel painful and frustrating to be pulled away from it. You may have had meltdowns or outbursts of frustration when this has happened.

How do you feel when you become absorbed in your spins? Circle any words describing your experience below, adding others in the space provided.

Absorbed	Excited	Soothed
Calm	Focused	_____
Curious	Joyful	_____
Energized	Motivated	_____

It's possible that people have criticized you for having collections or interests that they consider "distracting," "weird," or not "age-appropriate." As a result, you may keep your interests secret or stop engaging in them altogether (Price 2022). However, spins are a source of energy, motivation, and self-regulation. Spending time *in your spin* is essential to living well.

Being Captivated by Intense Passions in ADHD

If you are an ADHDer, you may tend to have quite scattered attention, especially when activities or topics are not interesting to you (Groen et al. 2020). However, these distractions can vanish when something ignites your curiosity and flips you into *hyperfocus mode*. In hyperfocus mode, your attention is wholly and powerfully engaged in what you are doing, often for hours at a time (Ayers-Glassey and MacIntyre 2021; Groen et al. 2020). When doing a deep dive on a new *hyperfixation*, you may become so focused that you forget to eat, drink, or go to the toilet.

One suggestion for why this happens is the dopamine theory of ADHD (Volkow et al. 2009). Dopamine is the feel-good neurotransmitter in your brain and is part of your inner motivation and reward system. This theory suggests that the ADHD brain uses up its dopamine resources very quickly and continually runs out. While later research has called this dopamine theory into question, when you focus on your interests, it feels intensely enjoyable—and can even feel like an addiction. In contrast, less interesting tasks are much more challenging and unpleasant, and you may tend to avoid them.

How do you feel when you are spending time on your hyperfixations? Circle any words describing your experience below, adding any others in the space provided.

Absorbed	Excited	Soothed
Calm	Focused	_____
Curious	Joyful	_____
Energized	Motivated	_____

Unlike monotropic spins, the attraction to hyperfixations can suddenly fade. If you lose interest, it may be impossible to reignite your curiosity. This can be frustrating and expensive if you start and stop many new hobbies or activities this way. However, if you are lucky enough to have a job that constantly presents you with novel and fascinating tasks that activate hyperfocus mode, you will never get bored by your work.

Overloaded Executive Functioning

Executive functioning is a set of interrelated and overlapping mental skills that work together to form your internal management system (Barkley 2020). Your executive functions develop from early childhood through adolescence and adulthood (Best and Miller 2010). They are essential for learning, achieving your goals, and organizing your life as an adult. Your executive functions give you the ability to:

- Start tasks and switch between them

- Organize, plan, prioritize, and make decisions

- Retain and use mental information (working memory)

- Maintain your attention

- Track the passing of time

- Control your impulses and urges

- Monitor what you do and understand the impact of your behavior on others

- Adapt when things change

- Regulate your emotions (an important function that we explore later on)

Executive functioning can be difficult for many neurodivergent people, but particularly for ADHDers, in whom these essential functions seem to become easily overloaded. Interestingly, some ADHDers with high intelligence seem to be able to compensate for gaps in their executive functioning, making their difficulties hard for others to see (Keezer et al. 2021; Milioni et al. 2017; Rommelse et al. 2016). They can leave assignments to the last minute and still get good grades, create systems to keep themselves on track, find ways to control distractions, and force themselves to get things done—often involving perfectionism and high levels of anxiety. However, these coping mechanisms are usually unsustainable in the long term. Eventually, when the demands of your environment outstrip your internal resources, achieving your goals and staying on top of daily tasks can become exceedingly difficult.

Each of the executive functions is outlined on the following pages. Consider your difficulties with executive functioning and place a checkmark against any items that reflect your experience.

Task Initiation and Switching:
The ability to start and switch between tasks. If this essential executive function is overloaded, you may have difficulty with:

- ☐ Leaving things until the last minute (procrastinating) or not doing them at all

- ☐ Completing mundane tasks such as household chores or paying bills

- ☐ Stopping something you are doing to start something else

- ☐ Restarting something when you have been distracted

- ☐ Feeling uncomfortable and irritated when you need to stop what you are doing

- ☐ Feeling a powerful need to complete a story, episode, or quest before you can start anything else

- ☐ Juggling competing tasks, finding this exhausting and overwhelming

Organizing, Planning, Prioritizing, and Decision-Making:

These are essential tools to get things done. If this executive function is overloaded, you may have difficulty with:

- ☐ Planning and prioritizing tasks and deciding what to do first

- ☐ Misplacing or losing items

- ☐ Maintaining a tidy and organized home or work environment

- ☐ Using calendars and diaries consistently

- ☐ Planning things such as social events or work projects

- ☐ Needing a lot of information and time to make decisions

Working Memory:

Functioning much like random access memory (RAM) in a computer, working memory allows you to hold information in your mind in order to use it for different purposes. If your working memory is overloaded, you may have difficulty with:

- ☐ Forgetting things if you do not do them straight away

- ☐ Becoming muddled by multistep processes

- ☐ Forgetting people's names as soon as they are spoken

- ☐ Losing track of conversations when there is more than one person speaking

- ☐ Multitasking or working on more than one project at a time

Attention and Focus:

Both ADHDers and Autistic people can find maintaining focus challenging. If your attention tends to be scattered, you may have difficulty with:

- ☐ Focusing on what people are saying if there are other noises around you

- ☐ Starting many things but having trouble finishing them

- ☐ Completing assignments and other projects

- ☐ Getting distracted in lectures, studying, watching movies or TV, or reading a book

- ☐ Missing key details or mishearing information

- ☐ Tending to get lost in your thoughts or zoning out

Tracking and Managing Time:

The ability to track and manage time are common difficulties described by ADHDers. If you have difficulty managing time, you may struggle with:

- ☐ Being on time for appointments or social events
- ☐ Estimating the amount of time needed to complete things
- ☐ Spending too long on some tasks and running out of time for others
- ☐ Making plans for the future

Impulse Control:

The ability to choose when or whether you respond to your urges allows you to pause and think before you act and stop yourself from doing unwise or unhelpful things. If you have difficulty controlling your impulses, you may struggle with:

- ☐ Doing things without considering the long-term impacts
- ☐ Spending a lot of money on new interests, hobbies, or online shopping
- ☐ Jumping into conversations at the wrong time
- ☐ Finishing people's sentences
- ☐ Waiting in a line or queue
- ☐ Losing your patience or speeding when driving
- ☐ Stopping yourself from responding to urges such as binge eating or gambling

Self-Monitoring:

The ability to notice your behavior and understand its impact on others allows you to change your approach to situations if needed. If you have difficulty checking your behavior, you may struggle with:

- ☐ Speaking too loudly or softly
- ☐ Speaking at the wrong time in a conversation
- ☐ Noticing that you have offended someone
- ☐ Losing track of how much of a task you have completed
- ☐ Reviewing your work and checking for errors
- ☐ Noticing your unhelpful habits while you are doing them

Mental Flexibility:

Mental flexibility is the ability to adjust your behavior, thinking, or approach when things change, and look at situations from different perspectives. This mental skill is needed for learning, building friendships, and progressing toward your goals. If you have difficulty with mental flexibility, you may struggle with:

☐ Getting stuck on a particular line of thinking

☐ Noticing when you need to stop talking

☐ Needing to finish something even if it is no longer helpful or relevant

☐ Feeling uncomfortable or upset when something unexpected happens

☐ Changing your plans to adapt to the situation

☐ Getting stuck in the details, unable to see the complete picture

☐ Seeing things from someone else's perspective

Review your responses above to find the executive functions that cause you the greatest problems day-to-day. Identify your top three areas of difficulty by placing a 1, 2, or 3 against the functions listed below.

Executive Function	Area of Difficulty?
Task initiation and switching sets	
Organizing, planning, prioritizing, and decision-making	
Working memory	
Attention and focus	
Tracking and managing time	
Impulse control	
Self-monitoring	
Mental flexibility	

Describe three upsetting or frustrating long-term consequences of your executive functioning often being overloaded.

1. _____

2. _____

3. _____

Many memes, TikTok videos, and YouTube videos highlight executive functioning difficulties in both serious and lighthearted ways. Seek out images or videos that reflect your experiences. Make a note of anything helpful you learn below.

_____

_____

_____

Whether you struggle in many areas of executive functioning or just a few, difficulties with executive functioning can cause ongoing frustration and widespread impacts on your life. In chapter 5, you will explore how to achieve your goals by harnessing your neurodivergent strengths, adjusting your priorities, using technology to support you, and enlisting help from others.

Experiencing the World and Yourself Through Your Senses

You interpret information from the world around you through your senses of vision, hearing, touch, smell, and taste. Many neurodivergent people are more sensitive to things like noise, bright lights, and certain textures, while others need more sensory stimulation to register an experience. At least 90 percent of Autistic people, and most ADHDers too, have differences in sensory processing (Belek 2019; Kamath et al. 2020), Your combination of hyper- and hyposensitivities forms a unique sensory profile that influences how you feel in different situations and how you interact with the world around you.

Being More Sensitive Can Lead to Sensory Avoidance

If you are hypersensitive to certain sensations, some experiences may be so intensely uncomfortable that they make you upset, angry, overstimulated, or overwhelmed.

Listed below are the senses with examples of sensitivities for each. Use this box to briefly describe any sensory experiences you find particularly intense, uncomfortable, disgusting, or distracting.

Senses	Examples	Your Sensitivities
Vision	*Mess, clutter, crowded places, bright lights*	
Hearing	*Loud, repetitive noises, certain music, sirens*	
Touch	*Being hugged, certain textures, clothing labels, tight clothes/ shoes, sand/dirt*	
Smell	*Strong perfumes, certain food smells*	
Taste	*Intense flavors, certain foods or drinks*	

Being in situations where you cannot escape uncomfortable sensory experiences can be extremely upsetting, so it makes sense that you would try to avoid them. This pattern of responding is known as *sensory avoidance*. Depending on your sensitivities, you may try to avoid specific foods or smells, textures, or clothing; visual clutter; long drives; noisy places, crowds, or shopping centers; or people touching you.

How often do you experience distressing or stressful sensory experiences? Circle one:

Never   Rarely   Sometimes   Often   Very Often   Always

What situations, people, or places do you avoid because they make you uncomfortable?

_____

_____

_____

Being Less Sensitive Can Lead to Sensory Seeking

If you tend to be hyposensitive to specific sensory cues, you may need sensations to be more intense to be aware of them. You may also not realize that you are uncomfortable until you are already becoming overwhelmed and irritated. You may even be approaching a meltdown but not understand why you feel this way.

Consider the situations where it takes you a long time to notice you are uncomfortable. Briefly describe any sensory experiences you do not notice until they are very intense.

Senses	Examples	Your Hyposensitivities
Vision	*Facial expressions, street signs, clutter, mess, when things need cleaning*	
Hearing	*Certain noises, not hearing someone call your name*	
Touch	*Clothing or shoes that are too tight or uncomfortable*	
Smell	*Bad smells, body odor, strong perfumes, something burning on the stove*	
Taste	*Foods taste bland, adding hot spices or salt to everything to taste it fully*	

If you tend to be less sensitive to sensory stimuli, you might seek out heightened sensory experiences. This is known as *sensory seeking.* You may enjoy crowds, loud music, firm hugs, robust flavors, crunchy textures, or the pressure of tight clothing. You may also need to stream podcasts or YouTube videos to stay focused while you are working.

How often do you need to add extra layers or intensity to your sensory experiences to feel calm, focused, or relaxed? Circle one:

Never   Rarely   Sometimes   Often   Very Often   Always

What kinds of situations, people, or places do you seek out because you appreciate the intensity of the experience?

_____

_____

_____

_____

Sensitivity to Your Internal World

Your ability to know what is happening inside your body relies on four other sensory systems. The first three, the *proprioceptive*, *kinesthetic*, and *vestibular* senses, help you understand the location of your body in space, keep your balance, and coordinate movement in your body. Many Autistic people have difficulties with coordination and clumsiness (known as *dyspraxia*) due to being less aware of information from these senses (Cassidy et al. 2016; Riquelme, Hatem, and Montoya 2016).

How often do you have difficulty with coordination and balance? Circle one:

Never   Rarely   Sometimes   Often   Very Often   Always

Interoception is the sensory system responsible for noticing the signals and sensations inside your body, such as your heartbeat, hunger/fullness, thirst, pain, the need to go to the toilet, fatigue/tiredness, and emotions. Approximately three-quarters of Autistic people have difficulty sensing their internal states using interoception (Fiene, Ireland, and Brownlow 2018; Price and Hooven 2018). Called *alexisomia*, being less sensitive to your inner sensations means that you will not notice these experiences until they are so intense that they cannot be ignored. You may forget to eat until you are starving or not realize you need to go to the toilet until your bladder is bursting (Fiene, Ireland, and Brownlow 2018).

Alternatively, if you are more sensitive to these sensations, you may notice even the tiniest changes in your body. Sensations such as hunger, pain, tiredness, or cold then become impossible to ignore and can be distressing. Having greater or lesser awareness of your internal sensations is linked to mental health problems such as anxiety, panic disorder, OCD, post-traumatic stress disorder (PTSD), depression, and eating disorders, as well as physical health problems such as dehydration, malnutrition, and heat exhaustion (Fiene, Ireland, and Brownlow 2018).

Place an X on each line to describe how intensely you feel your inner experiences.

Sensation	Low Intensity	High Intensity
Heartbeat	•————————————————————•	
Breathing	•————————————————————•	
Hunger	•————————————————————•	
Thirst	•————————————————————•	
Stomach fullness	•————————————————————•	
Heat	•————————————————————•	
Cold	•————————————————————•	
Pain	•————————————————————•	
Nausea	•————————————————————•	
Itchiness	•————————————————————•	
Bladder/Bowels	•————————————————————•	
Tickling	•————————————————————•	
Emotions	•————————————————————•	
Tiredness/Fatigue	•————————————————————•	

You can use feedback from your senses to help regulate your emotions, anxiety, stress, boredom, level of activation, and attention. Intentionally engaging your senses to upregulate or downregulate how you feel is a skill that will help you care for yourself more compassionately. We explore how you can use your senses to self-soothe in chapter 3.

Difficulty Understanding and Regulating Your Emotions

Your emotions are one of the neurobiological responses coordinated within your limbic system, which is a complex collection of brain structures that link together thoughts, memories, and emotions with motivation and behavior to give you essential information on how to respond to the world around you. You use your emotions to connect to others and keep yourself safe (Boone, Gregg, and Coyne 2020). However, emotion regulation is an area of significant difficulty for many neurodivergent people. Your ability to manage your emotions depends on your ability to:

1. Notice the internal physical sensations associated with emotions

2. Interpret these sensations and correctly label the emotions

3. Regulate and manage your emotions

The combination of difficulty noticing internal sensations and correctly labeling the associated emotions is known as *alexithymia*. Alexithymia can look quite different depending on which of these three skills you find challenging. Some people with alexithymia have difficulty noticing the sensations associated with their emotions because they are hyposensitive to interoceptive cues (Cerutti, Zuffianò, and Spensieri 2018). These sensations include having a choked-up feeling in the throat when upset, tension in the chest when anxious, and a sinking feeling in the stomach when embarrassed. If you tend not to notice these kinds of sensations, you may:

•   Present as relatively calm and unfazed most of the time

•   Not notice you are upset until you feel incredibly distressed

•   Suddenly explode in anger in a way that feels unpredictable to others

•   Try to avoid potentially emotional situations as much as you can

Place an X on the line to reflect how much you notice the physical sensations associated with your emotions.

I notice subtle physical sensations associated with my emotions, including when I am only slightly upset.

I do not notice the physical sensations associated with my emotions until I am distraught.

Other people with alexithymia feel powerful emotional sensations inside their bodies but have difficulty interpreting what these sensations mean. Not knowing how and why you feel so upset can increase your anxiety. If you have big surges of emotions but struggle to identify them, you may:

•   Feel frightened or overwhelmed by your emotions

- Not be able to predict and avoid your emotional triggers

- Become irritable, angry, and blame others when you feel upset

- Not know how to respond in an emotionally charged situation

- Need to use logic to work out how you feel, causing a lag between the event and your understanding of it

- Try to avoid potentially emotional situations as much as you can

How often do you have difficulty labeling your emotions? Circle one:

Never   Rarely   Sometimes   Often   Very Often   Always

How often do you use logic or reasoning to understand how you feel? Circle one:

Never   Rarely   Sometimes   Often   Very Often   Always

How often do you experience a delay between something happening and understanding how you feel about it? Circle one:

Never   Rarely   Sometimes   Often   Very Often   Always

Unfortunately, alexithymia is associated with a higher likelihood of depression, suicidal thinking, and self-harm (Cerutti, Zuffianò, and Spensieri 2018). Alexithymia applies equally to pleasant and unpleasant emotions, so it can result in you experiencing less joy and lower life satisfaction too (Preece et al. 2020).

Emotion regulation is an executive function that helps you navigate the everyday stresses of life and control how you react to conflict, change, rejection, and daily hassles. If, like many neurodivergent people, you have difficulty managing your emotions, you may find these overwhelmingly uncomfortable experiences. Check any of the following difficulties that reflect your experience of emotions.

- ☐ Having frequent mood changes and sometimes overreacting

- ☐ Feeling stuck in your feelings for extended periods

- ☐ Finding it hard to calm yourself down

- ☐ Having uncontrolled emotional outbursts (meltdowns)

- ☐ Internalizing your emotions and being unable to speak (shutdowns)

☐   Developing unhelpful habits such as skin-picking, hair-pulling, self-harm, gambling, or using drugs or alcohol to soothe yourself

How often do you have difficulty calming yourself down when upset or distressed? Circle one:

Never   Rarely   Sometimes   Often   Very Often   Always

Describe some of the unhelpful ways you can respond to your emotions, such as becoming irritable, lashing out at others, or using unhealthy habits to soothe yourself.

_____

_____

_____

_____

It is important not to judge yourself if you find your emotions challenging—many people do. But regulating emotions is a skill you can develop. You will have an opportunity to build your emotion regulation skills in chapter 4.

Social Expectations Based on Fairness, Equity, and Consistency

Generally, what our society defines as "appropriate" social behavior is based on what is easiest or preferred for non-neurodivergent people. Many neuronormative social rules are built upon social hierarchies and relationships. How you behave depends on your closeness to the person, your relative social status, and how much you want to develop the relationship. These rules can pose difficulties for neurodivergent people, who tend to base social expectations on equity, fairness, honesty, and consistency. Although you may learn to follow others' social rules, trying to fit into this culture can feel as if everyone else has downloaded a rulebook, but you are missing some crucial pages—or even the whole book.

Autistic and ADHDer social culture is rich and vibrant—and often breaks neuronormative social rules (Kanfiszer, Davies, and Collins 2017). In the table below, we have summarized some of the key neurodivergent social preferences. Circle or highlight the descriptions that best describe your preferred way of socializing.

Neurodivergent Social Preferences	Examples
Relationships are based on deep understanding, detailed sharing, and honesty.	Being scrupulously honest when answering questions about yourself, even if it casts you in a bad light Alerting people when something is broken, faulty, or could be improved Responding to personal questions with a detailed, thoughtful response
Emphasis on fairness, equity, and social justice. Belief that everyone deserves equal financial, political, and social rights and opportunities.	Speaking up when an initiative or plan could cause someone harm or is unfair Speaking up in support of disadvantaged people Supporting animal rights Giving money or time to a cause and not seeking recognition for this
Being consistent, following through on commitments, and doing what you say you will do.	Expecting that people will deliver on their commitments Following through with plans, sometimes even when the situation has changed Feeling uncomfortable with changes that are unexpected or were not agreed
Following clearly defined, fair rules that align with personal values and make logical sense.	Challenging rules that don't make sense or aren't fair, and refusing to follow them Asking for the reasoning behind decisions

Being willing to speak the truth, advocate for what is right, and refusing to participate in social politics can lead neurodivergent people to be seen as black sheep, outcasts, or troublemakers. You may feel torn between being open and honest and protecting yourself from being disliked or ostracized.

Briefly describe a challenge you have experienced as a neurodivergent person in a setting where following neuronormative social rules was expected. Then describe which set of social rules you were following.

_____

_____

_____

Closely monitoring yourself to fit other people's social expectations is draining. No matter how well you "perform," you may find yourself worrying about how you could have handled something better long after it is over (Black et al. 2023). In chapter 6, you will explore how to build relationships with people who accept and embrace you as you are.

Communicating Directly, Accurately, and in Detail

It has long been assumed that neurodivergent people have problems communicating effectively. But we now know that communication between two neurodivergent people is as effective as communication between two non-neurodivergent people, while breakdowns are more likely to happen between neurodivergent and non-neurodivergent people. This is known as the *double-empathy problem* (Crompton, Ropar, et al. 2020; Crompton, Sharp, et al. 2020). In reality, neither approach to communication is better; *everyone* shares equal responsibility for communicating effectively.

The table below summarizes some of the differences between the neurodivergent and non-neurodivergent approaches to communication, showing where breakdowns can occur. Circle or highlight the descriptions that best match your style of communication.

Neurodivergent Communication	Non-Neurodivergent Communication
Tends to use language literally. Focuses on the literal meaning of the words (semantics) to decide meaning. May find idiomatic expressions such as "feeling under the weather," "sat on the fence," or "take a leaf from my book" confusing. May not understand sarcasm.	More comfortable with the nonliteral use of language, including idiomatic phrases and metaphors. Able to identify when what is said differs from what is meant by reading nonverbal cues. Understands sarcasm.
Dislikes small talk; feels uncomfortable or bored in conversations that do not analyze topics deeply.	Comfortable using small talk to build social connections and establish social hierarchy.
Prioritizes spoken words over nonverbal cues to understand the meaning of what is being said. May use body language to express enthusiasm or interest.	Considers spoken words and nonverbal cues, including tone of voice, facial expressions, and body language, to determine the meaning of what is said.
Prefers detailed analysis of topics of interest (monotropic focus), building expertise, deep sharing, and learning new information.	Gives sufficient information to communicate meaning without adding as much detail or context. Comfortable talking about a range of topics without subject matter expertise.
Comfortable in wandering, tangential conversations that loop back to earlier points.	Prefers conversations that have a linear, logical flow.

Neurodivergent Communication	Non-Neurodivergent Communication
Talks quickly when excited about a topic or highly stimulated (verbal hyperactivity).	Talks at a consistent pace in most situations.
Gives direct, honest, and helpful feedback, saying precisely what they mean. Finds it very difficult to lie. May feel that not giving the entire story and all relevant information is untruthful.	Focuses on being polite by implying or gently hinting at what they mean rather than saying it outright. May feel more comfortable lying or giving only part of a story to preserve the social hierarchy or a relationship.
Demonstrates interest and empathy by sharing personal anecdotes that reflect similar emotional experiences.	Demonstrates interest by asking the person questions about their experience and empathy by commenting on how the person must have felt.
Tendency to share detailed personal information quickly once a relationship is established.	Avoids talking about oneself too much, viewing this as rude or self-absorbed. Shares personal information only with close friends and family.
Feels a strong need to tell a story from beginning to end, returning to the story if interrupted (need for completeness).	Willing and comfortable to stop discussing a topic and leave details incomplete if the conversation shifts focus.
Unable to speak when anxious, burned-out, or under stress.	Able to speak in most situations.

Communication breakdowns can be avoided when everyone takes greater care to understand each other. In chapter 6, you will explore how to find people who share your appreciation for honesty, detail, and in-depth analysis or fast-paced conversations.

Your Uniqueness Is Your Strength

It might feel strange to think about your strengths, given that so much of the public conversation about neurodivergence has focused on deficits and problems. However, you undoubtedly have many helpful abilities associated with your neurodivergence—even if you are unaware of them. Particular skills seem to be shared by many neurodivergent people (Cope and Remington 2022; Courchesne et al. 2020; Price 2022; Russell et al. 2019; Schippers et al. 2022), and recognizing your strengths can lead you to exciting hobbies or a rewarding career path.

Working as a clinical psychologist, I feel fortunate to be able to use my strengths in pattern recognition, use of language, and analytical thinking style every day. I struggle with loud noises, can be easily distracted in groups, and am quickly exhausted by small talk. So, it is perfect that my job involves sitting with just one other human, having deep, thoughtful conversations, developing a collaborative understanding of the problem, and planning a way to improve things. —Jennifer

In the following table, we have listed many of the strengths you can find among Autistic people and ADHDers. Place a checkmark against items that match your abilities, adding anything unique to you.

Common Neurodivergent Strengths	Yes, This Applies to Me!
Information Processing	
Attention to detail	
Categorizing and classifying data	
Remembering substantial amounts of information on topics of interest	
Ability to notice slight imperfections	
Sensitivity through all the senses, including subtleties in taste, aroma, and textures	
Memory for music or perfect pitch	
Visualizing data in three dimensions	
Thinking quickly in a crisis or emergency	
Systems Thinking	
Pattern recognition	
Creating rules and systems that make sense	
Problem-solving	
Organizing and structuring information	
Seeing the flaws in systems and knowing how to correct them	
Strategic, high-level analysis	

Common Neurodivergent Strengths	Yes, This Applies to Me!
Creativity	
Challenging conventions, being able to deviate from what is expected	
Innovation and originality, thinking "outside the box"	
Orthogonal thinking—drawing information from unrelated fields to create new perspectives	
Conceptual thinking	
Justice and Equity	
Focus on helping others	
Loyalty, honesty, and forthrightness	
Commitment to justice, fairness, and equity	
Preference for following fair rules	
Passion for animal and human rights	
Being Dynamic	
Taking the initiative	
High energy, passion, and enthusiasm	
Risk-taking	
Intense curiosity	
Spontaneity	
Being flexible and open to new ideas	
Responding quickly to changes	
Being socially outgoing	
Playfulness	
Approach to Learning and Work	
Subject matter expertise, being a specialist	
Self-directed learning, learning by doing	

Common Neurodivergent Strengths	Yes, This Applies to Me!
Ability to hyperfocus, often for extended periods	
Surges of productivity, producing a large amount of work	
Diligent work habits, perseverance	
Being consistent	
Thoroughness and completeness	
Other Personal Strengths:	

Now, using your answers above as a starting point, complete the following sentences:

The three personal strengths that I value the most in myself are _____,

_____, and _____.

The areas of my life where I use these strengths most are:

_____

_____

_____

If you struggle with this exercise, try not to feel disheartened. You may be more used to criticizing yourself than thinking about your strengths. As you understand yourself better, you may uncover new strengths and abilities. You can come back and add to this list at any time.

In the next chapter, you'll explore how your strengths and difficulties shape your experience of life and the challenges you face because you live in a society that does not fully accept your needs.

CHAPTER 2

Finding Self-Acceptance in a Society That Doesn't Fully Accept You

It is time to create a story that understands that diversity in all aspects of life is something that we need and that we cannot progress without difference. It starts with us.

—Chloé Hayden, *Different, Not Less*

Neurodiversity is part of the shared experience of being human. You are one person in eight billion, each of whom has unique skills, abilities, and experiences of the world. Unfortunately, our society does not always accept these differences or accommodate the needs of individuals. Being different continues to be pathologized, fueling unhelpful myths, and misinformation. As a result, neurodivergent people routinely experience microaggressions that can be subtle yet communicate harmful prejudice (Nadal 2019; Pierce 1970). On the surface, they may sound quite innocent, but microaggressions like these can feel very hurtful:

"Everyone is a little bit on the spectrum."

"It's just a fad. Everyone seems to have ADHD/Autism now."

"You can't have Autism because you can hold eye contact/are so good to talk to."

"You can't have ADHD because you finished school/have a job/degree…"

"Your symptoms just come from trauma."

"You can't have ASD because you are not like my cousin with Autism."

"You don't have ADHD; you just take on too many things."

"It's just an excuse."

These statements dismiss and invalidate your experience (Williams 2020). By trying to reassure you that you are "normal," they imply that being neurodivergent is something unwanted and shameful. They also communicate a broader expectation that everyone must meet specific standards to gain acceptance in our society, even though these expectations are often unattainable for anyone with a spiky profile of strengths and difficulties. You may have spent your life trying to achieve society's ideals even though it never felt quite right. If so, you might be surprised to learn that *you do not need to accept or strive to meet these expectations.*

In this chapter, you will explore the impact of negative attitudes and stigma on your wellbeing and the understandable but unhelpful coping strategies you may have developed. Letting go of other people's expectations will challenge you to unwind the unreasonable standards you've internalized and redesign your life according to your values and needs.

Before you go any further, we should warn you that what you read here might be slightly confronting. At times, you may feel overwhelmed by the challenges you face. Yet even though this might be uncomfortable, we encourage you to keep going. The first step in developing greater compassion for yourself is pausing to notice how you are struggling. By helping you understand the obstacles you experience, we hope you will come to appreciate that your difficulties are not your failures—it's society that has failed to accept and support you.

Pathologizing Differences Leads to Worse Outcomes

Modern medicine, including psychiatry, focuses on classifying, identifying, and treating symptoms and diseases. Medical researchers have developed many life-saving interventions and continue to make valuable breakthroughs in treating diseases every year. But when applied to neurodivergence, this approach has many limitations. By focusing on finding abnormalities, disorders, deficits, and dysfunctions and treating symptoms, the problem always lies within the person to be fixed.

The success of medical interventions is measured by how well the person can fit into the regular school environment, fulfill typical work requirements, or contribute to society. As a result, we still do not have a single therapeutic approach designed to improve the quality of life of neurodivergent people. Instead, we have problematic treatments (Bottema-Beutel et al. 2023) that:

- Train Autistic children to pass as nonautistic to others through rewards and punishments, including teaching Autistic children to hold eye contact and hug others without regard for their autonomy and choice.

- Train Autistic children in neuronormative social skills on the assumption that Autistic children cannot make social connections because they do not make friends or play in the same ways as other children.

- Teach Autistic and ADHDer children to behave better in class and not disrupt others by making them sit still ("quiet hands") and pay attention ("eyes to the front") without considering the negative impact on the child's ability to self-regulate and learn.

The dominance of the medical model can be seen in the millions of dollars spent researching genetics and cures when most neurodivergent people want acceptance and support (Bonnello 2022). Medical language also reflects this pathologizing approach (Radulski 2022), which perpetuates the negative stigma associated with Autism and ADHD. Unfortunately, although well meaning, the medical model has ultimately contributed to worse physical and mental health outcomes for neurodivergent people.

The Pervasive Impact of Minority Stress

As members of a stigmatized minority group, neurodivergent people are vulnerable to *minority stress*. Minority stress comes from persistent marginalization, discrimination, and exclusion. Its destructive impacts permeate every aspect of life, directly contributing to poorer life outcomes (Flentje et al. 2020). Autistic people and ADHDers experience greater frequency and severity of mental health problems, including higher rates of PTSD, depression, anxiety, suicidal ideation, psychiatric hospitalization, and completed suicide (Hedley and Uljarević 2018; Martini et al. 2022; Rumball et al. 2021). Neurodivergent people are also more likely to be unemployed, underemployed, or employed in roles beneath their abilities and have greater difficulty accessing healthcare, housing, and financial security (Radulski 2022; Sciberras et al. 2022).

Minority stress also contributes to a greater burden of chronic illness. Neurodivergent people are significantly more likely to have a large number of health problems, including autoimmune conditions, allergies, gastrointestinal disorders such as irritable bowel syndrome (IBS), chronic fatigue syndrome, sleep apnea, celiac disease, asthma, narcolepsy, dysautonomia including postural orthostatic tachycardia syndrome (POTS), Ehlers-Danlos syndrome (EDS), chronic pain and fibromyalgia, seizures, obesity, dyslipidemia, hypertension, thyroid disease, diabetes, vitamin deficiencies, strokes, Parkinson's disease, and more (Casanova et al. 2020; Croen et al. 2015; Csecs et al. 2022; Forde et al. 2022; Grant et al. 2022; Instanes et al. 2017; Owens, Mathias, and Iodice 2021; Tint et al. 2021; van Rensburg et al. 2018; Weir, Allison, and Baron-Cohen 2022). Unless we radically improve societal attitudes and reduce stigma, minority stress will continue to place a disproportionate burden on the health and wellbeing of neurodivergent people.

With such pervasive negative stigma, it's not surprising that parents, teachers, and health professionals continue to avoid giving children "the label," particularly as it is not yet well-known that educational, social, and work outcomes are considerably better for children who receive a diagnosis earlier in life (Belcher et al. 2022; Clark et al. 2018; Oredipe et al. 2023). Even a late diagnosis can significantly improve self-compassion, self-acceptance, and mental health in adults (Leedham et al. 2020; Lilley et al. 2022; Wilson et al. 2023).

We will only reduce stigma and achieve acceptance from society when the needs of neurodivergent people are treated as equal to those of non-neurodivergent people. To improve outcomes for all neurodivergent people, health professionals need to stop pathologizing difficulties and basing treatment on harmful stereotypes and instead recognize each person's unique information processing, sensory, communication, and social needs. Achieving this will take time and persistent advocacy. We hope that you can join us in supporting this change.

The "Dis-Abling" Effect of Intersectionality

People with disabilities are one of the world's largest minority groups (Lindsay et al. 2023); however, our social system is designed to make life easier for the majority, who are "en-abled" by this structure. As a member of a minority, society does not offer what is easiest for you, accommodate your differences, or provide support for your difficulties. This is "dis-abling" and why many forms of neurodivergence, including Autism and ADHD, can be considered a form of disability. *Ableism* is a pervasive form of discrimination against people with disabilities that consists of "beliefs and practices that devalue and discriminate against people with physical, intellectual, or psychiatric disabilities and often rests on the assumption that disabled people need to be 'fixed' in one form or the other" (Bottema-Beutel et al. 2021). Ableism contributes to disabled people having greater difficulty finding employment, underemployment, higher rates of poverty, poorer physical health outcomes, higher rates of mental ill-health, and lower overall quality of life (Friedman 2023; Lindsay et al. 2023).

Your experience of discrimination and ableism can be worsened if you are a member of multiple minority groups. *Intersectionality* is a term coined by Professor Kimberlé Crenshaw to describe how your individual characteristics, including race, gender, sexual orientation, wealth, education level, appearance, and health, expose you to overlapping forms of discrimination and marginalization (Crenshaw 1991). Your unique combination of identities will determine how vulnerable or accepted you are in different social settings and how you are treated in every area of society, including by healthcare providers. Your outcomes are likely to be worse if you are a neurodivergent person with overlapping forms of intersectionality, including being Black, Indigenous, or a person of color (BIPoC), because you experience racism in addition to ableism (Friedman 2023).

Many neurodivergent people also have identities that can be the target of discrimination and marginalization, including sexual orientation and gender expression. Autistic people and ADHDers are significantly more likely to identify as gender diverse and nonheterosexual (Strang et al. 2014; George and Stokes 2018). We don't know why these differences co-occur; it may be because neurodivergent people are less likely to conform to social expectations and thus are more open to exploring diverse sexuality and gender identities.

When I started to transition, I reevaluated everything I did based on whether it was "fem" or "masc." I wanted to express my feminine identity more, but I still didn't feel I fit in with other women. That is when I realized that I might also be Autistic. I had a speech delay when I was a kid and got lots of speech therapy, but no one ever told me I was Autistic. Because I was good at math and a quiet student, I think they didn't want to give me the label. So now I'm trying to understand how to live authentically as a woman and an Autistic person. It's a lot to sort out. —Sally

Consider your intersectionality and how this has influenced your experience of life. Below is a list of some of the aspects of intersectionality that exist in our society. Circle any that apply to you. Add any others in the spaces provided, or, if you prefer not to use these labels, describe your unique identity in the section for "other relevant identities."

Gender Identity	Sexual Orientation
Cisgender	Opposite-sex attracted
Nonbinary	Same-sex attracted
Transgender	Queer
Bigender	Questioning
Genderqueer	Straight/heterosexual
Agender	Asexual
Other:	Bisexual
	Other:

Color/Cultural Identity	**Education and Socioeconomic Status**
African	Level of education:
Asian	Family of origin income level:
Black	Low – Medium – High
European	Income level:
First Nations/Indigenous	Low – Medium – High
Indian/Southeast Asian	Housing status:
Latinx	
White/Caucasian	
Other:	
Medical Illness/Disability/Mental Health	**Physical Characteristics and Appearance**
Mental health diagnoses:	Body size, height, or proportions:
Chronic illnesses:	Skin coloration, scars, or birthmarks:
Chronic pain:	Attractiveness:
Other disabilities:	Conventionally Attractive – Average – Not Conventionally Attractive

Other Relevant Identities and Characteristics:

Consider how your unique intersectionality has influenced your experience of life. Place an X on the line to indicate how your intersectionality has either offered benefits or contributed to difficulties in your life.

Contributed to relative privilege   Contributed to greater difficulties

•——•

Striving for Ideals That Were Not Designed for You

Our social standards are based on the needs, desires, and comfort of the majority (den Houting 2019), and to be accepted, you are expected to work hard to meet them. The extent to which you are advantaged (abled) or disadvantaged (disabled) in society depends on the fit between the expectations placed on you by society, other people, *and yourself*, and your spiky profile of strengths and difficulties. Whenever the expectations placed on you are not adjusted to match your abilities, you will be unable to perform to your potential. However, you will thrive when you can capitalize on your strengths and your difficulties are accommodated.

When neuronormative societal expectations become the standards you set for yourself, you have *internalized ableism*. As you struggle to achieve these standards, you can develop a harsh and critical inner voice that, like a relentless fault-finding machine, judges you on how perfectly you "perform neurotypicality" (Price 2022). The list of things you can critique yourself for is endless. Trying to meet unattainable standards is exhausting and demoralizing, but the consequences of not meeting them can be much more painful.

Consider the social expectations you have for yourself that you don't always meet. Complete the following sentences with self-critical statements that reflect these expectations.

I should always _____

_____.

I should be better at _____

_____.

I am hopeless at _____

_____.

The problem with me is _____

_____.

Briefly describe the impact of this self-criticism on your mental health, confidence, self-esteem, and sense of achievement.

_____

_____

_____

_____

Self-compassion offers the potential to neutralize the effect of self-criticism. Self-compassion is founded on realistic expectations and acknowledging your limitations. By offering yourself support, self-compassion allows for practical solutions, highlighting your strengths and identifying where you need assistance. Complete the following as self-compassionate statements.

I am good at _____

_____.

Something I find difficult is _____

_____.

I need help with _____

_____.

A challenge I can overcome is _____

_____.

Briefly describe the potential impact on your mental health, confidence, and sense of achievement if you could speak to yourself more compassionately.

_____

_____

_____

_____

How Your Body Responds to Pervasive Stigma

Despite the incredible diversity of humankind, the basic structure of the brain and nervous systems has not changed since our early ancestors. The ancient parts of your brain still alert you to potential threats, drive you to get the resources you need to survive, and seek safety, soothing, and connection with others. Your threat, drive, and soothing/connection systems play a vital role in your survival; however, they can get out of balance due to the stress of living in our complex and disconnected modern society.

The Threat System: Keeping You Safe

Crucial to your survival, your threat system is largely controlled by your sympathetic nervous system. Finely tuned to potential danger, it bypasses rational thinking and keeps you safe by responding to threat signals with instantaneous "fight, flight, freeze, flop, or fawn" reactions. The ability of humans to use language to describe their experiences further amplifies and extends this process. When you think about potential threats and negative experiences in the past, your body cannot distinguish between these thoughts and physically present threats. Your body tries to protect you by reacting the same in either scenario, which means your body can go into fight-or-flight mode in response to a traumatic memory or worry that someone might hurt you in the future. Repeated experiences of discrimination, alienation, and microaggressions will keep your threat system activated. This chronic stress causes sustained exposure to cortisol, which can affect your health.

The Drive System: Striving to Achieve, Acquire, and Be Entertained

Beyond responding to immediate threats, your ancestors also needed to gain the materials and resources they needed to survive (Gilbert 2009; Steindl 2020). Access to food, water, a safe living environment, tools, and sex are all essential to flourishing as a community, and the dopamine pathways in the brain reward these achievements, which also confer social status, power, and pleasure. Spending time *in your spin* and doing activities that interest or challenge you are healthy ways to engage your drive system. However, you can also be pulled into unhealthy habits when they are designed to offer these rewards. Smartphone apps, notifications, social media, gaming, high-fat and high-sugar foods, gambling, and online shopping are all designed to keep you engaged in ways that can become problematic.

The Soothing/Connection System: Caring for Yourself with Compassion

When they had what they needed to survive and were safe from predators, your ancestors spent time relaxing, recharging, recovering, and connecting with each other. Humans were safest when they were part of a community that supported each other, and the parasympathetic nervous system developed to help humans "connect, rest, and digest" (Gilbert 2009). By contrast, modern society tends to be more fragmented and complex. We must work hard to connect with our community. Families are not always safe places to be. When you grow up with people who reject you, your soothing/connection system may not fully develop. Yet our bodies still have the same need to soothe and recover. We can achieve this by helping and caring for each other; in other words, through compassion.

Compassion is an active process that can flow in three directions: from you to others, from others to you, and from you to yourself (Kirby 2017; Steindl 2020). As a neurodivergent person, you may not have experienced much compassion from others. Instead, you may have faced harsh criticism, correction, and judgment for not meeting others' expectations and conforming to societal standards (Sciberras et al. 2022; Price 2022). Growing up this way can harden your expectations of yourself and others and affect your ability to give and receive compassion. Often, it is easier to be compassionate toward others than to receive compassion, although it might be difficult if you don't believe the person deserves kindness. The same principle applies to you. If you don't think you deserve compassion, offering it yourself can be challenging.

Self-compassion is an active process that activates your parasympathetic nervous system, enhancing your ability to self-soothe, self-regulate, and connect safely with others. Self-compassion uses the same skills needed to offer compassion to others (Kemp 2021; Kolts 2016). To get a sense of this, consider this scenario:

You are holding a newborn animal, perhaps a puppy, kitten, or chick. This fragile baby animal needs your care. You do not judge it for being vulnerable. Instead, you have tender feelings of warmth and kindness toward it. Being responsible for this animal's wellbeing feels a little uncomfortable because you are acutely aware of the risk that you could harm it by accident. Whether you feel the animal's fear inside your body or have a more thoughtful understanding of its experience, you feel a strong motivation to care for this tiny, fragile baby creature.

The skills you are using in this situation are the same as those needed for self-compassion: being non-judgmental and sensitive to suffering, having the motivation to help, and having the courage to sit with discomfort. Being compassionate also involves offering warmth and kindness in response to suffering (Gilbert 2009; Kolts 2016). You will have an opportunity to activate these skills and practice applying them to yourself in this book.

Living with the Threat of Rejection

Stemming from a lifetime of social misunderstandings, traumatic experiences, and criticism from others, along with difficulties in managing the uncomfortable emotions that come from these situations, *rejection sensitivity* is a powerful and long-lasting physiological response to feeling criticized, excluded, ignored, or rejected (Bedrossian 2021). Sometimes called rejection-sensitive dysphoria (RSD), rejection sensitivity is a challenge for many neurodivergent people. The pain of rejection feels so automatic, intense, and long-lasting, it suggests that your nervous system is treating rejection as a threat (Babinski et al. 2019).

Place an X on the line below to reflect how intensely you experience rejection.

Extremely upset and   Not at all upset or
overwhelmed by rejection   overwhelmed by rejection

•——•

Given how painful rejection can be, it makes sense that you would try to avoid it. There are three ways you might try to avoid painful rejection:

1. Hide who you are

2. Try to keep people happy all the time

3. Withdraw to keep yourself safe

These self-protective patterns can become so ingrained that it becomes difficult to imagine living any other way. Yet while they may keep you safe, they can also cause you other problems. Let's look at each in turn.

Hiding Who You Are

Trying to hide or camouflage your differences in order to pass as "normal" and avoid the negative consequences of not fitting in is called *masking* (Hull et al. 2017; Lai et al. 2017; Perry et al. 2022; Radulski 2022). Masking is a broad term that encompasses suppressing, camouflaging, and compensating for your differences. While most of the research to date has focused on masking in Autistic people, ADHDers are also likely to try to disguise their difficulties through masking (Kidwell, Clancy, and Fisher 2023; Syharat et al. 2023). The foundation of masking is suppressing your authentic self to fit neuronormative expectations. The aim is to appear "normal" by hiding aspects of yourself that may seem odd or unusual to others. Suppressing behaviors can include:

- Never sharing your opinions

- Not asking for what you need

- Controlling or hiding your urges, gestures, or mannerisms

- Hiding your enthusiasm for your interests

- Suppressing your sense of humor and urge to laugh

How often do you suppress your natural behaviors to fit in with others?

Circle one:

Never	Rarely	Sometimes	Often	Very Often	Always

Another approach to masking is called *camouflaging*. This strategy involves delivering a consistent social performance and requires conscious effort. Even if it feels unnatural and exhausting, you can become trapped into performing this version of yourself for others. Camouflaging behaviors include:

- Copying other people's gestures and mannerisms

- Portraying a more easy-going or happy persona

- Repeating famous quotes or in-jokes

- Laughing when you don't find something funny

- Asking questions to avoid talking about yourself

How often do you copy others or play a role to be liked by others?

Circle one:

Never   Rarely   Sometimes   Often   Very Often   Always

Compensating is the attempt to hide the specific difficulties associated with your neurodivergent spiky profile. Compensating behaviors can include:

- Holding eye contact even if it feels uncomfortable or distracting

- Controlling your urge to speak

- Changing your facial expressions, body language, or tone of voice

- Pretending to be interested

How often do you change your behavior to compensate for things you find difficult?

Circle one:

Never   Rarely   Sometimes   Often   Very Often   Always

Both men and women mask; however, women, those assigned female at birth, and nonbinary people may mask more (Lai et al. 2017; Radulski 2022). Masking can become so automatic that you may not even realize you are doing it (Livingston et al. 2020; Miller, Rees, and Pearson 2021; Price 2022).

Place an X on the line to reflect how automatic masking has become for you.

It's completely automatic; I'm not   It's something that always
aware I'm doing it   takes conscious effort

●————————————————————————————————————●

Unfortunately, masking has been linked to worsened mental health and wellbeing (Cassidy et al. 2020; Evans, Krumrei-Mancuso, and Rouse 2023; Hull et al. 2021). People who can successfully mask their differences and difficulties are also less likely to be given a diagnosis of Autism or ADHD when assessed (Lai et al. 2017). The more you can unmask and have others accept you, the more relaxed and at ease you will feel. In chapter 7, you will learn how to unmask safely and express yourself authentically.

Trying to Keep Everyone Happy

People-pleasing is a self-protective pattern to help you avoid rejection and emotional pain. Closely related to masking, this pattern is common amongst neurodivergent people and can take many forms. Here are some examples of people-pleasing behaviors. Place a checkmark next to any that apply to you.

- ☐ Agreeing to do things you don't want to do

- ☐ Feeling guilty or anxious if you have to say no, even to unreasonable requests

- ☐ Expressing enthusiasm even when you don't like something

- ☐ Agreeing to someone's plans without thinking

- ☐ Playing the peacekeeper role and patching up conflict

- ☐ Always trying to keep everyone in a good mood

- ☐ Doing things for people to earn their approval, friendship, or to be needed

- ☐ Pretending to be a certain way so people will like you

- ☐ Apologizing and taking the blame when something wasn't your fault

Briefly describe what people-pleasing has cost you in time, energy, emotional exhaustion, and mental and physical health.

_____

_____

_____

_____

_____

_____

Draw a picture of yourself as a strong, independent, empowered neurodivergent person who looks after their needs and expects others to treat them respectfully.

People-pleasing is a self-destructive process where your needs are never recognized. When you reinforce other people's unhelpful expectations of you, it can be hard to escape this pattern and it will contribute to burnout.

Withdrawing from Others

Withdrawing from others helps you avoid rejection by avoiding situations where you could be judged or criticized. Used when needed, withdrawing from others might simplify your life and help you recover from burnout. However, if you avoid people altogether, you will likely feel isolated and lonely.

How often do you withdraw from people to stay safe from rejection?

Circle one:

Never   Rarely   Sometimes   Often   Very Often   Always

Briefly describe any benefits you gain from spending time alone.

_____

_____

_____

Briefly describe any problems that develop when you withdraw from others.

_____

_____

_____

It might seem like you only have two options—be hurt or be alone—but there is a way to manage your sensitivity to rejection and safely spend time with other people. In chapter 4 you will learn skills that can help you manage the difficult emotions that come from rejection. In chapter 6, you will learn how to develop safe friendships, let go of people-pleasing, define your boundaries, and begin to say no.

Disability, Ableism, and the Use of Affirming Language

Within the wider disability rights and social justice movements, the neurodiversity-affirming movement is founded on the understanding that all kinds of human diversity deserve respect. Neurotypes are viewed as a social identity on a par with gender, ethnicity, sexual orientation, and disability status. The language used within the neurodiversity-affirming movement reflects this shift toward self-advocacy. You can model self-respect powerfully and simply through the language you use to describe yourself.

Reflecting this focus, the most dramatic change in the preferences of the neurodivergent community has been the shift from using person-first language ("I have autism," "she has ADHD") to identity-first language ("I am Autistic," "she is an ADHDer"). For many people, identity-first language is an act of radical self-acceptance, signaling that neurodivergence is integral to their identity and not something they want to change, hide, or fix (Shakes and Cashin 2020). However, not everyone prefers identity-first language. While it may be our preference, it is a valid personal choice if you wish to stick with a person-first language.

Another meaningful change has been abandoning the terms "high-functioning" and "low-functioning" (Bottema-Beutel et al. 2021). While never part of the formal diagnostic system, functioning labels have been used since 2013 when Asperger's syndrome was incorporated into Autism. Unfortunately, functioning labels tend to reflect internalized ableism (Bottema-Beutel et al. 2021). They also oversimplify a person's level of capability, placing it at a fixed level when we know that functioning fluctuates hourly, daily, and throughout your life.

Labeling someone as low-functioning can be very harmful when it contributes to someone losing their autonomy, but being labeled as high-functioning can also be damaging. Many people mask at work but collapse when they get home. Gifted children may perform well academically but have meltdowns when things change. Calling a person high-functioning can invalidate these genuine difficulties and communicate an expectation that the person must consistently perform at an exceptional level, which, in turn, encourages unhelpful masking.

The influence of the medical model still pervades the language we use to describe Autism and ADHD. "Casual ableism" may be delivered with good intentions, but offers pity rather than respect, focuses on difficulties not strengths, and uses disrespectful, dehumanizing, and condescending euphemisms such as "differently abled" or "special." Speaking up against ableism means calling out this language and the attitudes that come with it.

Consider language that has been used by others to describe yourself or a family member. Circle all that apply and add any others to the list.

Abnormal	High-functioning	Tragic
Deficit	Low-functioning	_____
Disordered	Pathological	_____
Dysfunctional	Special	_____

How do you feel when you hear these terms used? Circle any of the emotions listed, adding others relevant to you.

Angry	Helpless	Ridiculed
Anxious	Hopeless	Sad
Ashamed	Hurt	Uncomfortable
Confused	Ignored	Unimportant
Embarrassed	Indifferent	_____
Fearful	Invalidated	_____
Frustrated	Overlooked	_____

Complete the following sentence:

The three terms that make me feel the most invalidated are _____, _____,

and _____.

It can feel awkward whenever we change our language. We found this clunky at first as it differed significantly from what we learned in our training programs. However, we encourage you to consider using affirming language because we know that the language you use to describe yourself will influence your attitude toward yourself.

> Soon after I was diagnosed, I developed a dislike of the term "ASD." I understand that many still use this term, but as a late-diagnosed person, I feel like I'm being told I'm disordered rather than different. At first, asking my health professionals to change their language choices felt awkward and uncomfortable. However, it's become easier to make this request each time. I don't offer a long explanation; I simply say, "I prefer not to use the term ASD because Autism is a neurotype, not a disorder." No one has challenged me on this; instead, the response has always been curious and positive. —Jennifer

A Brief Guide to Neurodiversity-Affirming Language

The following table summarizes the current language preferences within the neurodivergent community and best practice in healthcare (Bonnello 2022; Bottema-Beutel et al. 2021; Monk, Whitehouse, and

Waddington 2022). Remember, you can use any language you like to refer to yourself. When talking to others, check their preferences; if in doubt, use terms that are least likely to offend.

Potentially Offensive	Neurodivergent Preferred	Rationale
Autism Spectrum Disorder

ASD | Autism, Autistic, Autistic neurotype | "Disorder" is unnecessarily medicalized and reinforces the idea that Autism needs to be fixed or cured. Unfortunately, we do not yet have an accepted alternative for ADHD. |
Autism Spectrum Condition	Autism, Autistic, Autistic neurotype	Replacing the term "disorder" with "condition" still evokes a disease model.
Asperger's syndrome, Asperger's, Aspie	Autistic	Asperger's is a term no longer used as a diagnosis. While some still identify themselves this way, others have abandoned it because of the apparent association between Hans Asperger and the Nazis and the potential for ableism by creating a hierarchy within Autism.
Comorbidity	Co-occurring	Comorbidity refers to a disease model. Co-occurring offers a more neutral choice.
Cure, treatment	Specific support or service	Neurodivergence does not need to be cured or treated as a medical problem.
Functioning (high/low)	Specific support needs, individual strengths, and differences	Global functioning labels can perpetuate ableist attitudes and communicate unrealistic expectations. It is more helpful to describe individual differences and support needs.
Normal person	Neurotypical, non-neurodivergent, allistic, nonautistic	Reflects the understanding that neurodivergent behaviors are different, not abnormal. As it can be hard to define neurotypical exactly, in this book we've mostly used non-neurodivergent.
Person with autism

Person with ADHD | Autistic person

ADHDer | Many prefer identity-first language because it emphasizes neurodivergence as inseparable from the person and an integral part of a person's identity. |
| Images of puzzle pieces, exploding brains | Any image that reflects positive attitudes toward neurodivergence | The use of puzzle pieces is associated with an organization that has promoted the tragedy narrative of Autism. Autistic people don't want to be viewed as a puzzle that nonautistic people must solve.

Exploding brain images may reflect a negative perception of neurodivergent capabilities. |

Potentially Offensive	Neurodivergent Preferred	Rationale
Restricted interests, special interests	Focused or intense interests, spins	Spin has been reclaimed by neurodivergent people to reflect their deep passions and interests.
"Suffering from" Autism or ADHD, images of people suffering, "tragic," "tragedy"	Is Autistic Is an ADHDer	Implying someone suffers because of their neurodivergence perpetuates the unhelpful tragedy narrative common in disability settings. Images of people suffering reinforce this narrative.
Symptoms, deficits, impairments	Specific neurodivergent experiences	Avoids medical terminology that assumes the characteristics of neurodivergent people are abnormal or deficient.

Consider the language people have used to describe you. How has it influenced how you feel about yourself?

_____

_____

_____

_____

_____

How could using affirming change the way you view yourself?

_____

_____

_____

_____

Take a moment to reflect on your use of language. Outline any changes you'd like to make by completing the following table.

What I Used to Say:	What I Will Aim to Say Instead:

Once you have decided on your preferred language, ask others to use these terms, too. Despite being best practice, professional uptake of affirming language has been slow, so we encourage you to tell your treating professionals the terms you'd like them to use to describe your identity. This is an example of "starfish advocacy"—small actions that contribute to shifting broader societal attitudes.

The people with whom I would like to share my affirming language choices are:

1. _____

2. _____

3. _____

4. _____

5. _____

Using affirming language to describe yourself is an essential step toward self-compassion. The next step will be to alleviate the burnout that inevitably comes from living in a world that does not accommodate your needs or accept you as you are.

CHAPTER 3

From Chronic Burnout to Living Well

Be kinder to yourself. And then let your kindness flood the world.

—Pema Chödrön

You feel exhausted, and no amount of sleep seems to make this any better. Simple tasks have become more demanding and drain your energy more. You feel foggy, can't concentrate, and keep forgetting things. It seems impossible to get organized; daily hassles feel overwhelming. Unfinished chores are piling up in your house. Even doing what you used to enjoy feels dull and drains your energy. You are more sensitive to loud noises, bright lights, strong smells, and scratchy clothing. Finding it difficult to be around people, you withdraw and isolate yourself. Some days, it's difficult to shower, clean your teeth, or wash your hair. Negative thoughts loop and swirl in your mind, and you feel like you are failing at life. You are in burnout.

Almost all of the Autistic people and ADHDers we see for therapy are in burnout when we first meet them. Even though burnout is a familiar experience for Autistic people and ADHDers, it remains poorly understood, and it can be challenging to distinguish burnout from mental health disorders (Arnold et al. 2023). On the surface, the signs of burnout can look quite similar to depression, generalized anxiety, bipolar disorder, borderline personality disorder, trauma, and even attachment difficulties (Iversen and Kildahl 2022). It is common to receive several incorrect diagnoses before learning you are in neurodivergent burnout (Au-Yeung et al. 2019; Iversen and Kildahl 2022). Of course, you can be in burnout *and* have other mental health problems too.

When neurodivergent burnout is the underlying cause of your problems, health professionals need to use a different approach to treatment. *Behavioral activation* is the standard, evidence-based treatment for depression and involves gradually taking on more as you resume your usual activities. However, when you are in burnout, attempts to increase your activity levels are extremely difficult to achieve and may worsen things (Raymaker et al. 2020). You could feel like you've failed therapy when the treatment has been targeting the wrong problem or you end up on medications that don't address the underlying cause of your difficulties.

In this chapter, you'll start your journey to recovery by understanding what burnout looks like and the causes of this often-chronic problem. You'll then learn how to recover and prevent burnout by noticing the early warning signs and choosing to treat yourself more compassionately.

Stuck in a Cycle of Burnout

Neurodivergent burnout is a common experience quite different from the burnout you experience in excessively demanding workplaces. Only recently has there been any research on this topic. So far, the primary focus has been on Autistic experiences. However, ADHDers are at risk of burnout too.

Are You in Burnout?

Everyone has a unique experience of burnout, but one thing is the same: it affects every aspect of your life. Burnout affects your sensory sensitivity, interpersonal stress, executive functioning, and emotional regulation. It also includes losing interest in your spins and worsening mental and physical health.

For me, burnout feels like the world is closing in on me. Everything feels overwhelming. Noises, smells, sounds, and lights all feel more intense. I feel profoundly fatigued and get more headaches. Any patience I had is gone. My thinking slows down as my brain stops processing any new information. Thinking about what I need to do is painful. I must lie in a cold, quiet, dark room, block out all my senses, and tune out from work. Talking is very difficult when I'm in burnout. I can read text messages but not respond, and I don't return phone calls or emails either. I know I'm really burned-out when I don't even want to focus on my special interests. Often, my burnout comes a day or two after a big event, but I still can't always predict when this will happen. —Monique

Place a checkmark against anything below that reflects a familiar experience for you. To understand your current state of burnout, place an asterisk (*) next to anything you have experienced *in the past week*.

Sensory Sensitivities:

☐   Increased sensitivity to external sensory experiences such as loud noises, bright lights, or crowds

☐   Increased sensitivity to internal sensory experiences such as pain, headaches, and fatigue

Interpersonal Stress:

- ☐ Losing the ability to mask or perform socially as others expect

- ☐ Being more blunt or irritable than usual

- ☐ Feeling overwhelmed by requests other people make of you

- ☐ Needing to avoid social situations, withdrawing from others

- ☐ Feeling unable to speak

Executive Functioning:

- ☐ Feeling completely overwhelmed by everyday tasks

- ☐ Increased forgetfulness and distractibility

- ☐ Having greater difficulty prioritizing, organizing, and getting things done

- ☐ Blurting out things that you later regret

Interests and Skills:

- ☐ Losing the skills needed for simple tasks

- ☐ No longer enjoying the activities you usually find rewarding

Emotion Regulation and Mental Health:

- ☐ Feeling emotionally sensitive

- ☐ More frequent meltdowns and shutdowns

- ☐ Feeling like you are failing and criticizing yourself for not meeting expectations

- ☐ Increase in habits like skin-picking, hair-pulling, nail-biting, or binge-eating

- ☐ Increased self-harm

- ☐ Increased thoughts of suicide

Physical Health and Wellbeing:

☐ Feeling exhausted in a way that is not relieved by rest or sleep

☐ Difficulties sleeping or poor-quality sleep

☐ Increased stomachaches, digestive issues, and worsening health overall

Take a moment to look over your responses. If you have checked quite a few of the items, you are likely to have experienced burnout. If you have placed an * next to many items, you are in significant burnout right now.

Burnout can be an acute, recurring, or chronic experience lasting from a few hours to many years (Mantzalas et al. 2022).

Acute burnout:	Feelings of complete exhaustion and overwhelm in the hours or days after a particularly demanding event such as a party or family gathering, work deadline, or exam, after which it takes hours or days to return to your usual level of functioning.
Recurring burnout:	Repeated episodes of acute burnout due to the same stressor(s) each time. Recurring burnout may happen at the end of each work/school day and can contribute to physical and mental health problems.
Chronic burnout:	Feelings of exhaustion and overwhelm that persist for months or years and include ongoing physical and mental health problems. This may include acute episodes where burnout deepens before returning to a chronic baseline. The length of recovery will depend on how deep your chronic burnout has become.

How often do you experience acute episodes of burnout?

Circle one:

Never   Rarely   Sometimes   Often   Very Often   Always

How often do you experience recurring episodes of burnout caused by the same stressor(s)?

Circle one:

Never   Rarely   Sometimes   Often   Very Often   Always

If you are in chronic burnout, when did this start?

_____

_____

Burnout can have potentially devastating consequences on every aspect of your life. Consider the impact burnout has on your ability to complete everyday activities, and indicate how much burnout affects your ability to complete daily activities by placing an X on each line below. Home administration includes paying bills, completing paperwork, and organizing repairs. Personal care includes showering, brushing your teeth, and washing your hair.

Activity/Task	No Impact	Significant Impact
Housework	•—————————————————————————•	
Home Administration	•—————————————————————————•	
Grocery Shopping	•—————————————————————————•	
Personal Care	•—————————————————————————•	
Exercising	•—————————————————————————•	
Eating Healthily	•—————————————————————————•	
Studying	•—————————————————————————•	
Working	•—————————————————————————•	
Seeing Friends	•—————————————————————————•	
Maintaining Relationships	•—————————————————————————•	
Accessing Health Care	•—————————————————————————•	
Going on Holidays	•—————————————————————————•	
Enjoying Hobbies	•—————————————————————————•	

Complete the following sentences:

When I am in burnout, the activities I find most challenging to complete are

_____, _____, and _____.

Describe the long-term impact of burnout on your life.

_____

_____

_____

_____

_____

Given what you now know, describe any mental health diagnoses you've received that could be explained by chronic burnout.

_____

_____

_____

You can deepen your understanding of burnout by listening to other people's stories. Search online and on your preferred video streaming platforms for terms like "autistic burnout," "sensory overload," "executive functioning overload," or "ADHD burnout." Look for personal stories and perspectives that reflect your experience. Make some notes about the key points that resonate for you below.

_____

_____

_____

_____

Explore your experience using the space below to draw what burnout feels like.

Consider sharing what you learn about burnout with a close friend or family member so that they can understand your difficulties better. They may even share their challenges with burnout too.

The Causes of Burnout

Simply defined, burnout occurs when the demands on you exceed your ability to cope. These demands can come from many sources. Sensory stressors, social hassles, organizational complexity, unwanted or unexpected change, emotional experiences, the need to hide your difficulties, a poor fit between your work and the challenges you experience because of your spiky profile, and not knowing you are neurodivergent are all factors that can contribute to burnout (Raymaker et al. 2020; Mantzalas et al. 2022; Phung et al. 2021).

Many neurodivergent people experience burnout when they reach a major life transition, such as finishing school, going to college, having children, or getting a promotion. At each significant stage of your life, expectations increase, and so does the load on your executive functioning. As you transition to adulthood, many parents also withdraw their support and expect their young adult children to quickly become more independent. At some point you may "hit a wall" and feel completely overwhelmed by so much change (Crompton and Bond 2022). Some people only experience burnout for the first time in their 30s, 40s, and 50s as they become overwhelmed by the competing demands of parenting, caring for aging parents, starting a business, studying while working, paying bills, cooking, cleaning, gardening, or maintaining relationships. Once in burnout, you cannot recover if the stressors continue to increase and you keep striving to meet unrealistic expectations without help (Arnold et al. 2023; Higgins et al. 2021; Raymaker et al. 2020; Welch et al. 2021).

Consider the points in your life when it became more challenging for you to manage. Place a checkmark next to any transitions that contributed to burnout for you.

- ☐ Starting elementary school

- ☐ Starting middle school

- ☐ Starting and finishing high school

- ☐ Attending college or other study

- ☐ Starting work

- ☐ Getting a promotion

- ☐ Moving out of your family home to live independently

- ☐ Moving homes, moving interstate or internationally

- ☐ Marriage/partnering

- ☐ Having children

- ☐ Working and parenting at the same time

- ☐ Relationship breakups/divorce

- ☐ Reaching an older age

- ☐ Perimenopause and menopause

At any stage of life, multiple factors can contribute to burnout simultaneously, making it difficult to know precisely what overwhelmed you. Below are some of the factors that can cause burnout at any time in your life. Check any that apply to you, and place an * next to the five factors contributing most to your current burnout.

☐ Needing to mask your differences, socially camouflage, or conceal your difficulties

☐ People-pleasing and poor boundaries

☐ Caring for others, particularly if they also have complex needs

☐ Lack of support, empathy, and accommodations from others

☐ Experiences of discrimination, bullying, trauma, and exclusion

☐ Interpersonal conflict and relationship breakdowns

☐ Sensory overload and overstimulation

☐ Boredom and lack of stimulation

☐ Excessive pressure from others, being expected to meet unrealistic standards

☐ Striving to achieve perfectionistic standards

☐ Poor health, chronic pain, and poor sleep

☐ Mental health problems, including isolation and loneliness

☐ Financial, housing, and employment stress, including being underemployed

☐ Unexpected life changes, accidents, and major health problems

☐ Executive functioning overload from taking on too many projects at once

☐ Too high workload

☐ Other: _____

☐ Other: _____

If you are a woman or were assigned female at birth, you can also experience acute burnout whenever your estrogen levels fall. Estrogen supports the brain's functioning and is involved in dopamine, serotonin, and noradrenaline production—all of which affect your mood. The amount of estrogen your body produces changes throughout your life, increasing during puberty and pregnancy and falling after childbirth, in perimenopause, and at menopause. Estrogen also rises and falls twice during each menstrual cycle, dropping quickly after you ovulate in midcycle. Every time your estrogen levels fall, your feelings of being overwhelmed may increase.

If you experience burnout in midlife for the first time, you may need to decrease your workload, get more support, and consider taking medications or hormone replacement therapy. Despite the pervasive effects of burnout, it is possible to recover. You can also prevent new episodes of burnout from becoming debilitating if you catch them early, take steps to reduce your stressors, and actively self-soothe.

Walking a Compassionate Path to Recovery

Neurodivergent burnout is a physical and mental health emergency. Recovery from burnout involves consistent, self-compassionate actions that address how overburdened you've become. It may also require significant life changes such as restructuring your work and home life, addressing relationship problems, holding boundaries, saying no to unreasonable demands, and gradually unmasking and expressing your authentic self.

In the following pages, you will explore neurodivergent-friendly strategies for alleviating burnout when it happens. You'll learn to recognize the early warning signs so that when you know burnout is coming, you can choose to self-regulate through your senses, absorb yourself in your interests, and look after your health. Caring for yourself in this way is an act of self-compassion essential for your long-term wellbeing.

Learn to Notice the Early Warning Signs

It is easy to spend your life preoccupied with your thoughts, stuck in analysis and thinking loops; however, to prevent burnout, you need to be aware of early warning signs in your body. Listening to your body can give you helpful information about how you feel and what you can do to feel better.

SENSATIONS MANY PEOPLE FEEL IN THEIR BODIES

Here is a list of some common physical sensations. Add any others that reflect your experience.

Activated	Energetic	Paralyzed	Teary
Agitated	Exhausted	Peaceful	Tender
Blank	Fatigued	Pounding	Tense
Breathless	Foggy	Prickly	Throbbing
Buzzing	Frozen	Queasy	Tight
Calm	Heavy	Relaxed	Tingly
Choked up	Hollow	Restless	Tired
Churned up	Hot	Rigid	Trembly
Clammy	Jumpy	Shaky	Twisted
Clenched	Lethargic	Sick	Twitchy
Crushed	Loose	Sinking	Warm
Detached	Light	Slowed	Weary
Dizzy	Lively	Sluggish	_____
Drained	Nauseous	Soft	_____
Dulled	Numb	Sparkly	_____
Empty	Pain	Sweaty	_____

With practice, you can develop your ability to notice these signals. Let's start by increasing your general bodily awareness.

Connecting with Your Body in the Present Moment

In this activity, you will have an opportunity to notice any physical sensations occurring in your body and follow this with a self-soothing activity. You will find an audio recording of this exercise at http://www.newharbinger.com/53073.

Begin this exercise sitting or lying or in any position that feels comfortable to you. Close your eyes and take several long, slow, deep breaths. Continue breathing slowly and gently, allowing your breath to gradually deepen without forcing it.

After a few minutes, when your breath has settled into a calm rhythm, mentally scan your body from your head to your feet, looking for any physical sensations such as tension, calm, tightness, heaviness, churning, agitation, pains, or restlessness.

Each time you notice a physical sensation, describe what you feel and where the sensation is in your body. Say this aloud using a quiet, gentle, and neutral tone. For example, "I feel tight in my chest," "I feel foggy in my head," or "I feel restless in my legs." Continue this way for several minutes, quietly describing each new sensation as you go. If you notice pain, acknowledge this aloud, then breathe gently through the sensation and continue with the exercise when possible.

After a few minutes have passed like this, settle into silence. Ground yourself by gently curling your toes and pushing your feet onto the floor. Listen to what your body needs to comfort and soothe itself. Notice whether your body needs to move, and if so, gently rock, sway, wriggle, bounce, tap your fingers, or stroke a soft pillow—whatever feels soothing for you. You may like to hum or sing to yourself. Whatever it is, absorb yourself in these gentle activities, doing whatever helps you to feel comfortable for as long as you like.

Notice what happens to any physical discomfort you are feeling in your body. Some of these sensations may gently fade away, while others may linger. Finally, when you are ready, acknowledge your effort in completing this activity and take several more long, slow, deep breaths. Gently bring this activity to a close by opening your eyes.

Using the list of common sensations as a guide, describe three physical sensations you noticed in this activity and where in your body you noticed them.

I felt:

_____ in my _____ , and

_____ in my _____ , and

_____ in my _____ .

Briefly describe any strategies you used to comfort, settle, or soothe your body. These may be helpful ideas for the future.

_____

_____

_____
_____

Listening to your body is the first step in understanding your experience better. It's a foundational skill for emotion regulation too. The better you get at interoception, the easier it will be to recognize the early signs of burnout. The following exercise may help.

Look for the Early Signs of Burnout

This activity builds on the last one by identifying the physical sensations that are your early signs of burnout. Practice this several times over the next week to fine-tune your ability to notice these sensations.

Think back to a recent experience you found so overwhelming and exhausting that it took you a long time to recover afterward. Describe:

Where you were: _____

_____

What you were doing: _____

_____

Who you were with: _____

_____

How you felt: _____

_____

Describe up to five factors that contributed to your burnout.

1. _____

2. _____

3. _____

4. _____

5. _____

Try to remember the physical sensations you experienced as you began to feel overwhelmed and overloaded and where these sensations were located in your body. (These sensations might also repeat as you remember the situation.)

Describe your early warning signs of burnout by completing the following sentence, noting each sensation and where you felt it in your body. For example, you might write "agitated (in my) chest and arms" and "throbbing (in my) head."

When I am approaching burnout, I feel:

_____ in my _____, and

_____ in my _____, and

_____ in my _____.

Over the coming weeks, watch for these specific physical sensations, as they may signal that you are beginning to get overwhelmed.

Understanding your warning signs will help you to recognize burnout sooner and take steps to self-soothe before it worsens. Three strategies can be helpful for this: making yourself more comfortable by reducing sensory stressors, regulating through your senses, and diving into your spins and hyperfixations. But before you can do this, you must make a clear decision to offer yourself care rather than criticism. Choosing a compassionate response to your struggle may be unfamiliar, but is a crucial turning point in your recovery from burnout.

Choosing to Offer Yourself Kindness

As soon as you notice you are beginning to burn out, you must remove yourself from the situation as soon as possible to slow down, rest, and find relief through your favorite self-regulation strategies. Check any strategies you might use to recover:

☐ Spend time in a quiet, dark room

☐ Wear noise-cancelling headphones or earplugs

☐ Stick to a simple daily routine

☐ Remove visual clutter to create a soothing environment

☐ Stick to safe foods and easy to prepare foods or takeout

☐ Wear loose, comfortable clothing

☐ Wrap yourself in blankets or tight clothing

☐ Spend time playing games, watching TV shows, or listening to music

☐ Spend time with your pet

☐ Take a break from social media

☐ Put off or ask others for help with basic chores

Since sensory stress is such a pervasive contributor to burnout, it's important to reduce your exposure to uncomfortable sensory experiences. Simple strategies such as wearing sunglasses, having dim lighting or the curtains closed, avoiding shopping, and wearing noise-canceling headphones or earbuds can all help. Over time and with patience, these small adjustments can reduce stress and help alleviate and prevent burnout.

Here are some of Jennifer's daily choices to be more comfortable when stressed or approaching burnout:

Sense	Adjustments
Vision	*Reducing visual clutter, wearing dark colors*
Hearing	*Keeping the TV volume low, wearing noise-cancelling headphones*
Touch	*Wearing comfortable shoes and loose clothing*
Smell	*Avoiding strongly scented perfumes, candles, and incense*
Taste	*Adding spicy flavors and salt to food to enhance the taste*

Now it's your turn. Complete the following table by describing small adjustments that could make you feel more comfortable.

Sense	Adjustments
Vision	
Hearing	
Touch	
Smell	
Taste	

Being kind to yourself in these simple ways may feel unfamiliar. However, learning to recognize your hesitancy and gently offer yourself kindness anyway offers a new pathway to nurturing yourself in the long term.

Overcoming Barriers to Self-Compassion

In this activity, you will uncover your barriers to offering yourself compassion and explore the possible benefits of developing these skills. Listed below are a range of common beliefs people have about self-compassion. Place a checkmark against statements reflecting your concerns, doubts, and fears about self-compassion. Add any others in the spaces provided.

Genuine fears, concerns, and skill gaps:

☐ Being kind to myself feels too unfamiliar, uncertain, or scary.

☐ Being self-compassionate would make me too weak, soft, or vulnerable.

☐ If I am self-compassionate, I might break down and lose control.

☐ I don't know how to be kinder to myself.

☐ It's too difficult to learn how to be self-compassionate.

☐ Other: _____

Learned unhelpful beliefs:

☐ Self-criticism is how I motivate myself—without this, I would be lazy and unproductive.

☐ I need to criticize myself to improve my performance and avoid mistakes.

☐ Other people will get upset with me if I show that I'm struggling or complain.

☐ Being hard on myself is what's expected.

☐ People won't like me unless I put their needs first.

☐ Other: _____

Self-judgments linked to emotional pain, shame, and guilt:

☐ Other people deserve kindness more than me.

☐ I am not worthy of self-compassion.

☐ Being kind to myself would be selfish, self-centered, and inconsiderate of others.

☐ I should be able to cope and sort out my own problems.

☐ No one else has shown me compassion, so why should I offer it to myself?

☐ Other: _____

Tally the number of checkmarks for each section and write down the scores below. Notice whether one area scores higher than the others or if your personal barriers exist across all categories.

Barriers	Score
Genuine fears, concerns, and skill gaps:	
Learned unhelpful beliefs:	
Self-judgments linked to emotional pain, shame, and guilt:	

Consider how you might have developed this way of thinking. Briefly describe any people in your life that you've watched be judgmental, harsh, and self-critical towards themselves and how their behavior may have influenced you.

_____

_____

_____

_____

Now, let's look at the reasoning behind each type of barrier in more detail.

Acknowledging Your Genuine Fears, Concerns, and Skill Gaps

Your score: _____

If you have no experience being kind to yourself, it is understandable that you would have concerns about what it would mean to be more self-compassionate. It's normal to struggle to do something new when the outcome is unknown, and you may find that your default response to such uncertainty is "No." Fortunately, there is a great deal of research showing that self-compassion supports better mental health and quality of life.

You've already started building self-compassion skills by deepening your understanding of the challenges you face as a neurodivergent person and acknowledging the difficulties that come with your spiky profile. You are also learning how to take small, compassionate actions to care for yourself. From here, go at your own pace, taking tiny steps to build these skills over time.

Briefly describe one way you could overcome your fears and concerns to build your skills in self-compassion.

_____

_____

_____

_____

Overcoming Learned Unhelpful Beliefs

Your score: _____

"Tough love" is a pervasive idea in Western society. If you have watched other people treat themselves harshly when they make mistakes, you may believe this is the only way to keep yourself on track. Yet you probably speak to yourself much more unkindly than you'd ever speak to someone else. If so, you might be bullying yourself. Self-criticism ignites your threat system and only makes you feel worse (Beaton, Sirois, and Milne 2020; Cai and Brown 2021; Cai et al. 2023; Farmer et al. 2023).

This "old school" approach to motivation simply doesn't work. In fact, it is much more effective to motivate yourself with encouragement rather than abuse, and speak to yourself with greater warmth while still holding yourself accountable. This may feel awkward at first, but with repeated practice, you can develop a more compassionate way of motivating yourself (Kemp 2021).

Briefly describe one situation where you would benefit from offering yourself more support.

_____

_____

_____

_____

Letting Go of Self-Judgments Linked to Emotional Pain, Shame, and Guilt

Your score: _____

When you are used to being scolded, criticized, and corrected, you can start to blame yourself when anything goes wrong. Over time, this can develop into a pervasive self-critical inner dialogue that is accompanied by powerful feelings of fear, guilt, shame, sadness, and resentment. You learn to label yourself as "lazy," "hopeless," or "stupid" and may believe that you are not worthy of kindness (Kirby 2017; Steindl 2020).

If this is how you've learned to speak to yourself, you may feel wary of self-compassion at first. Offering yourself greater kindness can bring to the surface sadness and regret about how you've been treating yourself and how others have treated you. If others have shamed you for speaking up or looking after yourself, you may feel uncomfortable doing that now. You are worthy of care and should not feel ashamed of your basic human needs. However, shame is a powerful emotion. If distressing and overwhelming feelings repeatedly show up as you work through this book, you may benefit from the additional support of an affirming therapist.

List up to six kind and supportive words you could use to describe your strengths, such as "persistent," "honest," and "practical."

_____   _____

_____   _____

_____   _____

Once you decide to treat yourself with greater kindness, you can start to make small, compassionate choices to look after yourself. Regulating how you feel through your senses and absorbing yourself in your interests are two ways that you can care for yourself compassionately.

Regulate Through Your Senses

Stimming is an endearing name for sensory self-stimulation and describes any behavior that helps you maintain your attention, control your urges, and manage your emotions through your senses (Kapp et al. 2019; Wise 2022). Stimming can also help you keep your composure in conflict situations, help you cope with worries and stress, and support your learning by helping you stay engaged and focused (Charlton et al. 2021).

Stimming consists of dozens of daily habits so automatic that you hardly notice that you are doing them. A good clue as to whether something is a stim is that you do more of it when bored, excited, anxious, or upset, which suggests that you are using it to regulate how you feel.

STIMMING OPTIONS THAT MANY PEOPLE ENJOY

You may be surprised by how many everyday behaviors can function as stimming. Listed below are some common stims. Underline your favorite stims and place an * next to the stims that are most effective in helping you calm and soothe yourself. You can download a handout of these stims at http://www.newhar binger.com/53073.

Movement Stims	
Bouncing your legs	Swinging your legs back and forth
Cracking your knuckles or toes	Opening and closing your hands
Wiggling your toes or fingers	Moving your jaw from side to side
Clicking your teeth together	Moving your ankles in a circle
Going for a long drive on a winding road	Nodding and moving your neck
Knitting, crocheting, sewing	Tiptoeing
Tapping your feet	Stretching, twisting your body, yoga
Twirling your hair	Rapid or hard blinking
Drumming your fingers, tapping rhythms	Jumping, bouncing, spinning
Tapping your fingers or fists together	Hand/arm flapping/waving
Tensing and relaxing your muscles	Pacing or walking in circles
Swaying, rocking	Long-distance running, doing sports

Touch, Sensation, and Pressure Stims	
Rubbing textures between your fingers	Eating crunchy foods
Giving/receiving a firm hug	Squeezing your hands
Wrapping yourself tightly	Washing your hands
Getting under weighted blankets	Rubbing your hands together
Wearing tight clothes	Pinching or biting yourself
Touching each finger to your thumb one at a time	Gently patting or tapping yourself
Biting your nails or cuticles	Rubbing your lips together
Running your hands through your hair	Running your tongue over your teeth
Stroking or pulling hairs	Clapping
Hugging yourself	Rubbing or flicking your skin

Vocal Stims	
Humming	Whistling
Singing	Clicking your tongue
Talking to yourself aloud	Repeating words, phrases, or sounds (echolalia)
Counting aloud	

Visual Stims	
Rewatching your favorite TV show	Watching soothing or satisfying videos
Looking at bright or sparkly lights	Watching cars, traffic, trains
Playing with kaleidoscopes or spinning toys	Coloring
Watching a ceiling fan	Completing puzzles
Looking at a clock or hourglass	Looking at patterns
Watching sunsets, stars, the moon	

Auditory Stims	
Listening to the same song on repeat	Clicking stim toys, pens
Focusing on rhythms, drumming	Listening to the whirring sound of a fan or motor
Popping bubble wrap	Tapping your fingers or nails
Listening to white or brown noise	Clicking your fingers
Listening to water sounds, rain, waves, ocean	Clapping

Taste & Smell Stims	
Seeking out strong flavors and spices	Sniffing perfumes or scented candles
Sniffing strong smells, such as coffee	Seeking out smells that remind you of comforting memories
Baking	
Cooking your favorite dish	

List any other stims you enjoy.

_____

_____

Complete the following sentence:

The stims I find the most soothing and regulating are _____,

_____, and _____.

Often dismissed as hyperactivity or disruptive behavior in ADHDers and described in an invalidating way in the Autism diagnostic criteria as "restricted, repetitive behaviors," there is still a negative stigma attached to stimming. Many treatment approaches have aimed to suppress stimming to make neurodivergent people appear more "typical" and reduce behaviors that are annoying or inconvenient for others. By early adolescence, most neurodivergent people receive a clear message that they should stop stimming (Charlton et al. 2021). Even those who don't may choose to stop as part of masking.

List any stimming behaviors you no longer use because you were embarrassed or told to stop by others.

_____   _____

_____   _____

_____   _____

How do you feel when people "correct" your behavior and tell you to stop stimming? Circle any of the emotions listed below, adding any others relevant to you.

Angry	Fearful	Ridiculed
Ashamed	Frustrated	Saddened
Confused	Hurt	Uncomfortable
Dismissed	Invalidated	_____
Disrespected	Irritated	
Embarrassed	Overlooked	_____
		_____

Stimming is normal, healthy, and an act of self-compassion. Given the potential stigma, it is understandable that you might choose to keep your stimming private. However, suppressing or swapping your natural stimming for less noticeable behaviors is usually less effective for self-regulation and can cause other problems. Children who reduce their stimming in early childhood experience greater anxiety as they get older, with one recent study finding that 94 percent of these children met the criteria for an anxiety disorder by the time they were 11 years old (Waizbard-Bartov et al. 2023). For this reason, we encourage you to actively seek out and use a wide range of stimming strategies to help you recover from and prevent burnout. Focusing on your stim, rather than just mindlessly doing it, may also enhance its ability to soothe and regulate your feelings.

Connect to the Present Moment Through Mindful Walking

In this activity, you will use walking to regulate how you feel while deepening your awareness of the present moment. If walking is not available to you, focus on some other repetitive movement with your hands or body. Prepare yourself by thinking about the words you would use to describe each step of the process; for example, you could describe the process of knitting as "insert – wrap – pull – slip."

You can complete this activity in shoes or barefoot. You may like to set a five-minute timer to know when to stop the activity. You will find a recording of this activity at http://www.newharbinger.com/53073.

Find a space where you can walk in a small circle without bumping into things. Start in a standing position, looking down at your feet. Pick up one foot and then slowly take one step forward. As you place your foot down, notice the sensation on each part of the sole of your foot as it touches the floor. Label in your mind or say aloud each part of your foot as they touch the floor, "heel, middle, toes." (If you toe walk, it may be in the opposite order, which is fine.)

Repeat this process with your other foot, slowly raising it off the ground, then slowly taking a step, noticing the sensation as your foot touches the floor and labeling each part of the sole of your foot as it touches the ground: "heel, middle, toes."

Repeat this process as you walk slowly in a circle, developing a gentle rhythm. If you get distracted, refocus on the sensation in each foot as it touches the floor and the labeling process. As you become more comfortable, you may like to lower your eyelids and block out the external environment even more to increase your focus on mindful walking.

Notice any emotions generated during this practice. If you notice any doubts or embarrassment, reassure yourself that you are safe to stim. Remind yourself that it's essential to look after yourself in this way.

Keep walking for as long as you want. When you are ready, or the timer goes off, finish your mindful walking by coming to a gentle stop. Pause and take a moment to acknowledge the time you've spent practicing mindful walking.

Circle the words below that describe how you felt during this activity. Add any others in the spaces provided.

Absorbed	Energized	Thoughtful
Activated	Focused	Uncomfortable
Awkward	Joyful	_____
Calm	Peaceful	
Embarrassed	Soothed	_____
		_____

Describe how you might use simple repetitive activities like walking to regulate how you feel.

_____

_____

_____

Strategies such as mindful walking offer an opportunity to benefit from an everyday experience. These opportunities are all around you—the key is finding the best strategies for you.

Absorb Yourself in Your Interests

No matter what they are, connecting with your spins and hyperfixations is a helpful self-regulation strategy for recovering from burnout (Parenteau et al. 2023). Even if you find it difficult to focus or concentrate on your interests due to fatigue, finding ways to incorporate them into your daily life is essential.

My special and intense interests are the center around which everything in my life revolves. Essentially, my special interest is collecting information about certain topics. Over my life, I've had strong and intense interests in animals, nature, horses, psychology (of course), medicine, health, yoga, spirituality, and history.

I have an intense drive to spend time focused on my interests every day and feel unfulfilled if I don't have time to do this. Luckily, my job revolves around my core interests, and most of my friends are also interested in the same things. —Monique

Many spins and hyperfixations revolve around understanding how things work, finding and appreciating patterns or systems, and collecting things that can be categorized or organized. This makes sense given that so many neurodivergent people have strengths in pattern recognition and systems thinking. The activities you use for self-regulation will depend on whether you need something energizing or calming.

SPINS AND HYPERFIXATIONS SHARED BY MANY NEURODIVERGENT PEOPLE

Activism, social justice

Aircraft, aviation

Animals (including pets)

Anime, animation, cosplay

Architecture, interior design

Art, painting, drawing, graphic design

Astrology, tarot, psychic

Beauty, makeup

Biology, ecology, flowers, plants, insects

Birds, bird watching

Books in specific genres or series

Cars, buses, trucks

Cartoons, comics, manga

Celebrities, actors

Craft, knitting, crochet, sewing

Dinosaurs, paleontology

Fashion

Forensic science, true crime

Games, gaming

Geology

History

Lego

Literature, language, poetry

Machines, robotics, engineering

Mathematics

Medicine, human biology

Model-making

Movies, specific studios, or genres

Music, musicians

Natural history

Perfumes/scents

Physics

Psychology, neuroscience

Role-playing

Ships, boats

Space, astronomy

Sports

Superheroes

Technology, coding, machine learning

Trains, transport systems

TV shows

War, history, aircraft, machinery

Yoga, meditation

Take a moment to think about what fascinates you and create a list below. Return to these spins and hyperfixations any time you need to recover, reenergize, and soothe your stressed-out nervous system.

My Short-Term Hyperfixations	My Long-Term Spins

When you are in burnout, you may prefer to connect with your interests in ways that do not require too much effort or energy (low-demand approaches, such as reading, watching videos, or arranging your collections). Alternatively, if you need greater stimulation, you might want to dive deeply into your interests, start a new project, or actively research new ideas.

Low-demand ways I can engage with my spins and hyperfixations include

_____, _____, and _____.

Active ways I can engage with my spins and hyperfixations include

_____, _____, and _____.

Imagine a Perfect Day Absorbed in Your Interests

Sometimes, you can't easily access your spins. This activity offers a way to self-regulate using your interests even when they are not directly available to you. You can complete this activity sitting, lying, or standing. You can find a recording of this activity at http://www.newharbinger.com/53073.

Gently close your eyes or lower your gaze. Allow your breathing to settle into a slow, deep, natural breathing rhythm. If you are sitting, feel the support of the chair and allow your body to settle and soften. If you are standing, gently curl your toes to feel the ground beneath you. Notice how your body stacks on top of your feet, like a set of building blocks rising from the ground. Gently wriggle your body to become aware of how it feels in space.

Think about spending uninterrupted and unlimited time in one of your favorite interests or activities, something that is a source of continuing fascination for you. Notice how it feels to be able to focus on this without constraints. Notice any pleasant physical sensations and warm emotions inside your body. You might visualize this with a warm, soft, nostalgic glow as if you were watching an old movie. Allow a gentle smile to form on your face. Breathe in deeply and slowly three times. Soak up the joy you experience with each breath.

You can end this activity here, or release your body to express your emotions. Allow yourself to move freely—bounce on your toes, spin, jump, sway, rock, wriggle, dance, flap, swivel, or twist—to express how you feel about your spin through your movements.

Spend as much time doing this as you want. Then, as you bring this activity to an end, gradually slow and bring your body gently back to a state of calm. Take a moment to capture this joyful, energized feeling so you can bring it with you for the rest of your day.

Describe any emotions and physical sensations you noticed inside you as you imagined spending uninterrupted time in your spin.

_____

_____

_____

_____

Describe the sensations you noticed when you released your body to express your emotions.

_____

_____

_____

_____

You don't need a lot of time or money to experience the pure joy and sense of satisfaction that comes from absorbing yourself in the things you love using your imagination and body.

Care for Your Body

Unfortunately, when you are in burnout, it becomes more challenging to care for yourself. The impact of this on your health can be significant. Burnout can affect your immune and digestive symptoms, trigger migraines, and worsen pain. If you neglect basic self-care needs, such as brushing your teeth, and do not seek help for medical problems, your health can deteriorate, adding to the burden of burnout.

List any health and self-care needs you tend to neglect when you burn out.

_____   _____

_____   _____

_____   _____

It's crucial to your recovery to meet your basic health needs. Do your best to look after your physical body by:

- Prioritizing sleep and rest

- Gently stretching your body

- Hydrating yourself with water or your favorite drink

- Brushing your teeth at least once a day or using mouthwash

- Setting reminders to eat, drink, and take your medications

- Buying simple, nutritious, premade meals

- Aiming to wash your hair once a week

- Using dry shampoo, deodorant, and wipes to meet your basic hygiene needs

- Asking someone to help you attend health appointments and take medications

If no one can help you look after yourself, you must be your own carer. Try to care for yourself with the same nonjudgmental attitude and generosity that you would offer to a much-loved relative or pet who is unwell. Remember that your physical health needs are valid and important—and that you deserve as much nurturing and support as anyone else.

List up to four small steps you can take to look after your physical health when in burnout.

_____   _____

_____   _____

Recovering from burnout starts with noticing the early signs of burnout and in that moment, choosing to care for yourself. Each time you do this, you are practicing self-compassion. While you may not be able to avoid burnout altogether, understanding what causes it and responding quickly will sometimes allow you to stop burnout from becoming debilitating and prevent the need for a prolonged recovery.

However, if you continue to experience the same stressors that led you to burnout, no amount of self-care will be enough for you to recover fully. Even taking a week or two of vacation will not be enough. Lasting recovery requires you to make multiple daily decisions to care for yourself with greater kindness and warmth. In the following chapters, you will explore how to create a life where your needs are met and you feel fulfilled and supported. This is the long-term antidote for burnout.

CHAPTER 4

Managing Your Overwhelming Emotions

No one ever shamed themselves into better mental health.

—K. C. Davis, *How to Keep House While Drowning*

You feel agitated, restless, and tense. Your stomach is twisting, and you feel a headache brewing. Feeling out of control, you don't know what to do. You have a powerful urge to escape right now and feel like you need to shout or cry, but you can't. It's hard to find the words to describe how you feel. Sometimes you get irritated by the people around you, even if they are not to blame, or you go quiet and withdraw, as if you are hiding inside your body. You need people to leave you alone, in quiet and darkness. These overwhelming feelings keep interfering with your life no matter what you try.

Navigating powerful emotions, meltdowns, and shutdowns is challenging, especially if you struggle to find the words to describe your experience. In this chapter, you will explore the origins of your emotions and how to soothe them when they feel out of control. Please note that this process opens with a frank discussion of the causes and consequences of emotional regulation problems, including trauma, addictions, meltdowns, and self-harm. If this content is too distressing for you right now, skip to the last section in this chapter, *Manage Your Emotions with Compassion.* You can come back at any time.

Why Are Your Emotions So Intense?

If you find your emotions frightening, overpowering, intense, and uncontrollable, there may be some significant stressors that are triggering these emotional experiences. Let's explore what these might be.

Exposure to Sensory Stressors

One challenge that can be easy to overlook is the impact of having an extremely sensitive nervous system. The *sensory stressors* that trigger emotional reactions can be anything—most of us have something we find intensely uncomfortable. You may find being around a lot of people incredibly draining, or be irritated by traffic or construction noise, or a loud voice coming from the room next door. Perhaps you cannot relax when the house is messy, the lights are flickering, someone is wearing strong perfume, or you feel hungry, nauseated, cold, or in pain. If you have *misophonia*, you will have difficulty tolerating some everyday sounds such as pens clicking, ticking clocks, tapping fingers, crinkling plastic, chewing, breathing, sniffing, or slurping, and find these unbearable and intensely irritating (McGeoch and Rouw 2020).

> *I'm in my car outside the supermarket, screaming and shaking. I am so tired after work, and shopping for groceries has pushed me over the edge. I can't move other than rocking in the car seat. A voice in my head tells me I am "putting this on," that I am "weak," and "I just want attention." I start thumping my head, and my body starts to twitch. Then I realize what's happening—I'm having a meltdown.* —Anna

Being in the presence of your sensory stressors is not something you ever "get used to." No matter what it is, if you cannot escape or alleviate it, your central nervous system will perceive the sensory stressor as unsafe and activate your threat system, leading you to panic, explode in anger, or shut down. Sadly, your level of discomfort only increases with repeated exposure.

Review the sensory sensitivities and insensitivities you listed in the section *Experiencing the World and Yourself Through Your Senses* in chapter 1. Then, for each sense listed, describe the sensory experiences that make you feel intensely irritated, anxious, or distressed.

Vision: _____

_____

Hearing: _____

_____

Touch: _____

_____

Smell: _____

_____

Taste: _____

_____

Internal body sensations (interoception): _____

_____

Balance and movement (proprioception, vestibular): _____

_____

Overburdened Executive Functioning

The Autistic brain tends to prefer certainty, predictability, and consistency, while the ADHD brain tends to need novelty and challenge. Depending on your unique spiky profile, the tension between these needs can feel chaotic. Racing, looping, tangled, tangential, and scattered thinking can make it hard to get organized. Staying focused and on track takes constant effort. Sudden changes can overwhelm you. Since managing your emotions is an executive function, your ability to regulate your emotions will also be affected as you become overburdened by daily demands.

Place an X on each line to describe how you feel in the following situations.

Situation	Calm, Confident, and Accepting	Embarrassed, Agitated, or Irritated
Unexpected events	•————————————————————————•	
Changes to your plans	•————————————————————————•	
Making a mistake	•————————————————————————•	
Forgetting something	•————————————————————————•	
Being distracted	•————————————————————————•	
Running late	•————————————————————————•	
Saying something wrong	•————————————————————————•	

Hyperempathy

Hyperempathy is the experience of intensely feeling other people's emotions mirrored within your body, which can heighten how you experience your own emotions. Hyperempathy may help you understand and connect with others, but it can also cause problems when others' intense emotions significantly affect yours. While joy can be contagious, being with someone who is intensely angry, sad, or frightened may also produce overwhelming emotions in you.

Being hyperempathetic may also make you more prone to developing anxiety, depression, and compassion fatigue (Leonard and Willig 2021). If you are hyperempathetic, you may find being around others overwhelming and need time alone to process and regulate your emotions. Working in a job that exposes you to people with intense emotions can also contribute to burnout.

Place an X on the line to reflect how much you are affected by other people's emotions.

I do not feel other people's
emotions unless I think
about them.

I feel other people's emotions
intensely and automatically
inside my body.

If you are hyperempathetic, list up to four of the emotions in others that affect you the most.

_____ 　_____

_____ 　_____

Interpersonal Stress and Rejection

For many neurodivergent people, relationships can be a significant source of stress, worry, and pain. Indeed, many of the most emotionally painful experiences occur in our relationships with family, friends, and intimate partners. Conflict, criticism, teasing, and losing friends can all be extremely painful.

Place an X on each line to describe how you feel in the following situations.

Situation	Calm, Confident, and Accepting	Embarrassed, Agitated, or Irritated
Being criticized	•————————————————————•	
Being teased	•————————————————————•	
Put-downs and jokes	•————————————————————•	
Being left out/ excluded	•————————————————————•	
Conflict and arguing	•————————————————————•	
Losing a friendship	•————————————————————•	
Being lied to	•————————————————————•	
Being pressured	•————————————————————•	
Being bullied	•————————————————————•	
Hearing gossip about you	•————————————————————•	

Briefly describe a situation when a relationship with a friend negatively affected your emotions.

_____

_____

_____

Traumatic Experiences

Neurodivergent people experience much higher rates of interpersonal trauma than non-neurodivergent people (Cazalis et al. 2022; Peleikis, Fredriksen, and Faraone 2022; Reuben, Stanzione, and Singleton 2021) and can develop trauma symptoms from a broader range of experiences, many of which don't meet the criteria for PTSD (Rumball, Happé, and Grey 2020; Rumball et al. 2021). Your *trauma load* consists of the cumulative impact of unprocessed emotions and negative self-evaluations that come from these experiences.

Place a checkmark next to any of the following experiences that may have contributed to your trauma load.

☐ Bullying from peers, teachers, or family

☐ Experiencing or witnessing abuse and domestic violence

☐ Interpersonal conflict and social stress

☐ Death of a caregiver, friend, other relation, or pet

☐ Mental health crises and breakdowns

☐ Physical illness, both acute and chronic

☐ Hospitalizations, both voluntary and involuntary

☐ Own or parents' divorce or conflict

☐ Exposure to injury or violence against yourself or others

☐ Having your body's autonomy not respected, such as being forced to do things against your will or to comply with treatments as a child

☐ Other: _____

The effect of trauma on your body can be profound; your threat system becomes stuck in "fight, flight, freeze, or flop" patterns that sensitize your nervous system, alter your beliefs about yourself, and heighten your emotional reactions. Trauma symptoms include panic attacks, intrusive thoughts and images, nightmares, feeling constantly on edge, and powerful emotions of shame, guilt, anger, and horror. These experiences can appear unexpectedly and feel so intense that you *dissociate*, an automatic response in which you feel disconnected from your body, and the world around you feels unreal. Episodes of dissociation can last minutes, hours, or much longer.

Briefly describe how your trauma load affects your ability to manage your emotions.

_____

_____

_____

_____

The higher your accumulated trauma load, the more challenging it can be to regulate your emotions in the presence of sensory stressors, other people's emotions, and interpersonal stress. Practicing the strategies described here will help you build the foundations of emotion regulation; however, you may also benefit from seeing a trauma-informed and affirming licensed therapist for longer-term support and recovery from trauma.

When Your Emotions Become Overwhelming

Emotional experiences can feel frightening when you can't control them and calm yourself down. It's understandable that you would try to avoid feeling this way by pushing down or "bottling up" your feelings or trying to distract yourself. You might also pretend to be happy to hide your feelings from others, or you may choose to isolate yourself from people altogether. Sometimes, focusing on helping others or asking people questions deflects attention from you. These strategies may help in the short term; however, eventually your emotions can become too big and persistent for you to push aside. This is when you can spiral into a meltdown or shutdown.

Meltdowns

Meltdowns result from a buildup of stress over a prolonged period. As tension grows in your body, it floods with adrenaline, making you increasingly agitated and restless. During a meltdown, you may feel completely overwhelmed, lose control of your emotions, have a powerful urge to lash out at others, or turn your anger toward yourself.

When I have a meltdown, I go on a rapid downward spiral. It can happen fast, usually starting when I think about everything I've missed out on in life. My friends have gone to college, got jobs, and are now getting married and buying houses, but I don't feel like I've achieved anything. If my mum is around, I often lash *out and shout at her. She doesn't know how to cope with me when I'm in this place and never says the right thing. In reality, there's nothing she can say that would help at that moment. It takes me a long time to recover, and I can feel drained for days.* —Lynne

Shutdowns

A shutdown originates in the same stressors as a meltdown, but instead of externalizing how you feel, you increasingly withdraw from your surroundings as you become overwhelmed (Phung et al. 2021). Shutdowns can vary in intensity and duration. In a partial shutdown, you feel emotionally empty but can still walk around, talk to others, and complete basic tasks. By contrast, in a complete shutdown, you feel totally numb, become nonverbal or minimally verbal, and cannot resolve the situation, describe how you feel, or ask for what you need. You may have to limit your usual daily activities and spend more time in bed.

I tend to respond to overwhelm by shutting down and becoming numb. My mind kicks into gear and will analyze the situation to help me escape. I may not realize something has upset or made me angry for hours or days. I usually need time alone in bed reading to recover and minimize social interaction. Unfortunately, shutting down has sometimes meant people do not recognize that I am distressed. They often tell me I am very calm, but that is not always my internal experience. —Monique

When your emotions are surging, it is natural that you would look for a strategy to calm yourself and give you back a sense of control—even if this strategy is physically painful or damaging to your body. Three unhealthy coping patterns that are common among neurodivergent people are body-focused repetitive behaviors, addictions, and self-harm.

Body-Focused Repetitive Behaviors

Many neurodivergent people struggle with body-focused repetitive behaviors (BFRBs) that include nail-biting, skin-picking, and hair-pulling. Often starting in childhood, BFRBs can help to regulate uncomfortable sensory, social, and emotional experiences and can calm "noisy" thinking—making them exceedingly tricky to stop (Charlton et al. 2021; Houghton et al. 2018; Kapp et al. 2019; La Buissonnière-Ariza et al. 2021). BFRBs are such strong urges that it can feel as if this is the only way you can get relief, even if you feel remorse later.

Listed below are some of the more common body-focused habits. Place a checkmark against any habits you have had in your lifetime and an * next to any *current* issues. Add any other habits in the space provided.

Skin-picking (excoriation):

- ☐ Pimples
- ☐ Blackheads
- ☐ Skin bumps
- ☐ Hair follicles
- ☐ Scabs
- ☐ Dry skin
- ☐ Cuticles
- ☐ Lips
- ☐ Nose

Biting:

- ☐ Nails
- ☐ Lips
- ☐ Inside cheeks
- ☐ Tongue
- ☐ Fingers

Hair-pulling (trichotillomania):

- ☐ Head hair
- ☐ Eyelashes
- ☐ Eyebrows
- ☐ Facial hair
- ☐ Arm, leg hair
- ☐ Chest/back hair
- ☐ Ingrown hairs
- ☐ Pubic hair
- ☐ Chewing/swallowing pulled hairs
- ☐ Hair cutting

Other:

- ☐ Thumb-sucking
- ☐ Knuckle-cracking
- ☐ Binge eating
- ☐ Other: _____

Usually unwanted, BFRBs can be an attempt to remove imperfections such as "bad" hairs, bumps on the skin, or pimples. You may also have an overwhelming urge to make things smooth or symmetrical, making it hard to stop until it feels "right." An important part of the experience can be the sensation of pulling, squeezing, or scratching, which can sometimes feel pleasurable or offer relief. These behaviors are often automatic and mindless, so you may not realize what you are doing until you have already done some painful damage to your body. If your habit causes chronic infections, bald spots, stomach problems, or scarring, you may feel reluctant to attend school, go to work, or socialize because of how your body looks and feels.

Describe the negative impact of BFRBs on your life, including any temporary or permanent damage to your body.

_____

_____

_____

Try not to judge yourself harshly if you cannot stop these patterns. Such habits can fade for months or even years, yet reappear at times of stress, exhaustion, anxiety, conflict, burnout, or boredom.

Addictions

Any activity or substance that provides a surge of dopamine and relief from your uncomfortable emotions has the potential to become an addiction (Karaca et al. 2017; Kervin et al. 2021). Addictions to alcohol, illicit substances, prescription medications, gambling, gaming, pornography, shopping, sex, and food can all be significant problems for neurodivergent people. Over time, getting the same surge of dopamine-related pleasure or relief becomes more challenging, making you need more of the substance or activity to get the same effect. This can make your addiction escalate.

For something to be considered an addiction, you need more and more of the experience to get the same thrill or benefit, and you find it difficult to reduce or stop. The activity or substance must also cause significant life problems that affect your financial security, housing stability, relationships, ability to work or study, or physical or mental health. Knowing this can help you distinguish an addiction from monotropic spins and hyperfixations. For example, if you enjoy collecting figurines, toys, or models associated with your spin, this is not a problem. However, if you are spending so much money that you are experiencing financial stress or accumulating debt, your house is filling up with clutter, or you leave the boxes unopened once the enjoyment of the purchase is over, you are likely to have a compulsive shopping addiction.

Briefly describe any addictions you have experienced in your lifetime and the negative impact they have had on you.

_____

_____

_____

Learning to regulate your emotions is essential to overcoming an addiction. However, if you are struggling with an addiction, we encourage you to seek specialist help as well. The recovery journey can be long, and you will need ongoing support.

Self-Harm

During meltdowns and shutdowns, self-harm offers a way to distract yourself from emotional pain, take control of your emotions, and bring you back to the present moment. It can also be a way of punishing yourself. Self-harm can include a wide range of behaviors such as pinching, biting, cutting, burning, scratching, or hitting yourself; hitting your head against the wall; or punching the wall. Some types of self-harm leave no permanent damage; others can leave permanent scars and cause health problems. If self-harm gives you much-needed relief, it can escalate over time. Although these habits might seem to offer relief in the short term, finding safer ways of regulating your emotions is important.

(Optional) Briefly describe the negative impact self-harm has had on your life, including any temporary or permanent damage to your body.

_____

_____

_____

Although they are frustrating and distressing, BFRBs, addictions, and self-harm are understandable responses to intense, unwanted emotions. Even if you successfully stop these patterns, until you develop other ways to self-soothe and reduce your overall emotional distress, there is always the risk that these habits will come back. So, let's explore the skills you need to do this.

Managing Your Emotions with Compassion

Having healthy and sustainable ways to manage your emotions is essential to a fulfilling life. Fortunately, it is possible to ride big emotional waves while looking after yourself and managing how you react. As we explored in chapter 1, managing your emotions depends on your ability to (1) notice the internal physical sensations associated with emotions, (2) interpret these sensations and correctly label the emotions, and (3) regulate the emotions to calm yourself down. You may be more skilled in some of these areas than others.

Let's explore five crucial steps to manage and regulate your emotions. These steps form an acronym, PRIMA (*first* in Italian):

1. **Pause:** Take a moment before you react

2. **Regulate:** Self-soothe through your senses and interests

3. **Identify:** Find the words to describe how you feel

4. **Meaning:** Listen to what the emotion is telling you and consider how to respond

5. **Allow:** Acknowledge your emotions and let them pass

As you work through each step, you will have opportunities to develop these skills. Remember to be kind to yourself and not expect perfection. Each skill will need practice to develop and time for it to feel natural for you.

Pause Before You React

On the verge of having a meltdown or shutdown, your first priority must be keeping yourself and everyone else safe. You can do this by pausing before you react and taking immediate action to care for yourself. If you can, leave the distressing situation until you can calm down. You may ask a trusted support person to help with this by teaching them to recognize signals that you are no longer coping, so they can help you calm yourself down.

> *When I'm having a meltdown, I can't talk, but my partner knows to turn the lights down and make the house quiet. She has seen this many times. I don't suppress the urge to let my body rock. It takes hours for me to use words again, but she doesn't pressure me. Prediagnosis, an episode like this might have stretched for days. Now, it's only a few hours because I know what's happening, and people around me know what to do. I feel much safer.* — Anna

Create a Safety and Self-Soothing Plan

It can help to prepare a plan for whenever you reach overwhelming distress (Wise 2022). Complete the following table to develop a plan for situations where you feel emotionally overwhelmed and need to take steps to keep yourself safe.

Safety Plan Steps	Example	Your Plan
Signs that I am becoming overwhelmed:	I feel the urge to avoid others, feel heightened sensory sensitivity, or become agitated or anxious.	
Signs that I am becoming overwhelmed that people might see:	I become more irritable, am unable to answer questions, and want to be alone.	
Things I can do to self-soothe and keep myself safe:	Find a quiet and safe space and give myself time to self-soothe by listening to music and stimming.	
When I am feeling overwhelmed, other people can help me by:	Not asking me a lot of questions, keeping the house quiet, giving me time alone and a favorite comfort item, and checking on me occasionally.	
People I can ask for help:	My mom Best friend My support worker	

Once you are safe, the next step is to help your body calm down so that you can begin to think rationally, work out how you feel, and decide what to do next.

Regulate and Self-Soothe

Your recovery starts the moment you realize that you are no longer coping. Even though you might be very agitated at the time, you can make a self-compassionate choice to care for yourself. There are three broad compassionate strategies you can use to help regulate your emotions: (1) focusing on your breath using a simple activity called *soothing rhythm breathing*; (2) active, intentional stimming; and (3) engaging in your spins and hyperfixations.

SOOTHING RHYTHM BREATHING

Sometimes, breathing exercises are given to help control anxiety. However, the purpose of soothing rhythm breathing is not to control how you feel but to activate your soothing/connection system. Soothing rhythm breathing is a self-regulation strategy that is always available to you. Even if you've tried breathing to reduce your anxiety and not found it helpful, we encourage you to try using soothing rhythm breathing. It can help you steady yourself when feeling overwhelmed, regulate your nervous system, and help you think more clearly. Practicing for a few minutes daily can help lower your baseline stress level and positively affect your wellbeing.

Soothing Rhythm Breathing

To develop effective skills in soothing rhythm breathing, find a time of day when you can practice for approximately three minutes. If you have difficulty paying attention to your breathing, hold an object such as a smooth stone or something that has a pleasant texture, and focus on this as well as your breathing throughout the activity. You will find a recording of this exercise at https://www.newharbinger.com/53073.

Settle into a comfortable position with your eyes closed or looking down to the floor. You may like to have the lights turned down in the room. Allow yourself to have a gentle facial expression or small smile to connect you to the compassionate part of yourself.

Begin to focus on your breath. Allow the air of each breath to come down into your diaphragm. You may like to place a hand on the bottom of your rib cage and feel it move in and out with each breath.

Without forcing it, *gently extend and deepen each breath. Gradually slow the speed of your breathing until you find a comfortable, soothing rhythm. There is no right or wrong way to breathe. What matters is that your breath gradually deepens and slows. Feel the air flowing in and out and your lungs expanding and contracting. Continue to focus on your breathing, allowing it to find a peaceful, soothing rhythm.*

Minds are much like kittens or puppies—when left to their own devices, they wander off. When you notice that your mind has wandered, gently guide it back to awareness of your breath. Continue with your breathing in this way for several more minutes.

As you finish, notice where your body is resting and the support of the chair, bed, or floor underneath you. Let yourself feel held and supported. Take this moment to appreciate the time and effort you've given to this activity and that you've cared for yourself in this way. Then, when you're ready, slowly open your eyes and bring yourself back to the present moment. Have a stretch and take one last deep breath to prepare yourself for the rest of your day.

Describe any changes or sensations in your body that you noticed during this activity.

_____

_____

Briefly describe how practicing soothing rhythm breathing could be helpful for you.

_____

_____

Finally, make some recommendations about when you could practice soothing rhythm breathing in the future and how you might remember to get this done.

_____

_____

_____
_____

SELF-SOOTHE WITH STIMMING

Stimming is essential to activate your body's soothing/connection system. If you are likely to self-harm or engage in your BFRB when overwhelmed, you may benefit from finding ways to meet your need for repetitive movement. Keep your hands busy with stim toys, fidgets, and activities that require fine motor skills, such as knitting, crocheting, drawing, coloring, sewing, painting figurines, gaming, and assembling models at times when you're more likely to do BFRBs, such as while watching television or sitting at your desk. Many "cozy" games on handheld gaming devices and your phone are emotionally regulating and keep your body moving in ways that are not destructive, distressing, and painful.

Review the list of *Stimming Options That Many People Enjoy* in chapter 3, then list up to six stims you can use when you feel emotionally distressed.

_____   _____

_____   _____

_____   _____

Consider creating a *sensory safe space* to access your sensory soothing strategies whenever needed (Wise 2022). Use a basket or drawer to hold your favorite stimming items and anything else you need to regulate, such as blankets, pillows, beautiful pictures, and scents.

DIVE INTO YOUR INTERESTS

To increase the impact on your emotions, spending soothing time in your interests can be combined with stimming to enhance the positive impact. For example, you could sing along with the soundtrack to your favorite show or dance energetically to your favorite music. You may prefer to find low-demand ways to enjoy your spins when you are emotionally overwhelmed, such as sorting or arranging your collections or putting headphones on to listen to your favorite podcast or music.

List up to six activities related to your interests that are helpful when you are emotionally upset. Include a mix of activating and low-demand activities.

_____   _____

_____   _____

_____   _____

Identify How You Feel

To understand your emotions, you will benefit from learning a broader vocabulary of emotion words and being able to recognize how they feel in your body. Emotions generally fall into the broad categories of happiness, sadness, anger, disgust, fear, and surprise (Rosenberg and Ekman 1995); however, within these categories there are many specific emotions, each with a different intensity.

Following are emotion words clustered in broad categories. To develop your emotional fluency, start by choosing the category of emotion, then search for a way to describe how you feel, matching this with physical sensations. You may like to return to *Sensations Many People Feel in their Bodies* in chapter 3 for ideas.

CLUSTER 1: HAPPY, CONTENT, GRATEFUL, HOPEFUL, LOVING

Possible words to describe these emotions:

Accepting	Delighted	Kind	Satisfied
Admiring	Desirous	Loving	Secure
Adoring	Ecstatic	Lucky	Sensual
Affectionate	Elated	Lustful	Serene
Amused	Empathetic	Optimistic	Sympathetic
Appreciative	Encouraged	Passionate	Tender
Awestruck	Enthusiastic	Patient	Thankful
Balanced	Fortunate	Playful	Touched
Blessed	Fulfilled	Positive	Trusting
Calm	Grateful	Present	Understanding
Caring	Happy	Proud	Warm
Centered	Hopeful	Relaxed	Wishful
Compassionate	Infatuated	Romantic	Wondering
Connected	Inspired	Safe	Worthy
Content	Joyful		Yearning

Typical sensations associated with these emotions include feeling light, warm, relaxed, and calm in your chest and whole body.

CLUSTER 2: SURPRISED, CURIOUS, ENERGIZED

Possible words to describe these emotions:

Brave	Energized	Fascinated	Powerful
Competent	Engaged	Interested	Shocked
Confident	Excited	Intrigued	Surprised
Curious	Determined	Involved	Stimulated

Typical sensations associated with these emotions are feeling buzzing, energetic, and trembling anywhere in your body.

CLUSTER 3: FEARFUL, ANXIOUS

Possible words to describe these emotions:

Afraid	Doubtful	Petrified	Tense
Alarmed	Fearful	Powerless	Terrified
Anxious	Frightened	Reluctant	Timid
Apprehensive	Helpless	Scared	Trapped
Concerned	Hesitant	Shocked	Uneasy
Confused	Nervous	Skeptical	Unsure
Dismayed	Overwhelmed	Stunned	Vulnerable
Disturbed	Panicked	Suspicious	Worried

Typical sensations associated with these emotions are feeling agitated, restless, queasy, hot, or tense.

CLUSTER 4: SAD, DISAPPOINTED, DISCONNECTED

Possible words to describe these emotions:

Anguish	Disappointed	Hopeless	Pained
Depressed	Dissatisfied	Hurt	Sad
Despair	Distant	Indifferent	Unhappy
Despondent	Empty	Lonely	Upset
Detached	Forlorn	Lost	Useless
Disconnected	Gloomy	Melancholy	Withdrawn
Discouraged	Heartbroken	Numb	Worthless

Typical sensations associated with these emotions are feeling hollow, numb, choked up, exhausted, tense, heavy, and paralyzed.

CLUSTER 5: ANGRY, HOSTILE, IRRITABLE

Possible words to describe these emotions:

Aggravated	Cranky	Exasperated	Irritable
Agitated	Cynical	Frustrated	Moody
Angry	Disdainful	Furious	Outraged
Annoyed	Disgruntled	Grumpy	Resentful
Bitter	Disturbed	Hostile	Upset
Contemptuous	Edgy	Impatient	Vindictive

Typical sensations associated with these emotions are feeling hot, shaky, agitated, and tense, particularly in your head and chest.

CLUSTER 6: DISGUST, SHAME, GUILT, REGRET

Possible words to describe these emotions:

Ashamed	Guilty	Jealous	Remorseful
Disgusted	Horrified	Mortified	Shamed
Embarrassed	Humiliated	Regretful	Sorry

Typical sensations associated with these emotions are feeling sickened, nauseated, heavy, or tightly clenched, particularly in your stomach.

CLUSTER 7: EXHAUSTED, FATIGUED

Possible words to describe these emotions:

Bored	Burned-out	Drained	Fatigued
Burdened	Depleted	Exhausted	Worn out

Typical sensations associated with these emotions are feeling heavy, weary, empty, or lethargic throughout your whole body.

Knowing how you feel when it happens is an extremely helpful skill. If you cannot immediately identify your emotions, try working backward by identifying the physical sensations first and then matching these with your emotions.

Tracking Your Emotions and Physical Sensations

Using the preceding list of words as a guide, over the next week try to notice up to three different emotions each day and at least one physical sensation that goes with each. You can download a blank worksheet for this activity at https://www.newharbinger.com/53073.

Day	Emotions	Physical Sensations
Day 1		
Day 2		
Day 3		
Day 4		
Day 5		
Day 6		
Day 7		

Look over your responses and complete the following statements:

The emotions that I noticed most often were:

_____   _____

_____   _____

_____   _____

Alternative words to describe these emotions more precisely are:

_____   _____

_____   _____

_____   _____

Using a broader vocabulary of words to describe your experiences and matching them to how you feel inside your body can help you understand your emotions better. You can use this knowledge to decide what to do next. To build this skill, try to practice it as often as you can.

Meaning and Purpose

Emotions often come with a strong urge to do something; what you do is always your choice. Whenever an overwhelming emotion is puzzling you or you feel a strong urge to react, it can be helpful to map out what the emotion might be trying to tell you (Boone, Gregg, and Coyne 2020). You'll need to pause and observe your big emotions to hear what they are saying.

The next time you have an intense emotional reaction, use the following worksheet to explore your reactions and decide how you want to respond. You can download a blank version of this worksheet at https://www.newharbinger.com/53073.

Questions	Example Situation	Your Situation
What is the situation?	I'm arguing with my girlfriend.	
What physical sensations do you feel in your body?	Agitated, choked up, tense, heavy.	
What thoughts are running through your mind?	Is she going to leave me? I never get things right.	
What emotions are you noticing?	Anxious, fearful, sad.	
What are your emotions telling you?	That I'm scared of losing the relationship.	
What urges do you feel?	I want to shout, cry, and run away.	
Is this an urge you want to follow? Will it result in a good outcome?	Not really. It's okay to cry, but shouting or running away will make things worse.	
What will you do?	Give myself time to calm down, then speak to her.	

At first, it may not be easy to work out what your emotions are telling you. Talking it through with a trusted friend might help you make sense of what's happening and give you another perspective to consider.

Acknowledge Your Emotions and Let Them Pass

The last steps in learning to manage your emotions are being willing to feel them and then letting them pass by. It can be difficult to allow yourself to experience your emotions if you've tried to ignore or avoid them in the past. Unfortunately, the more you run, fight, or hide from your emotions, the more uncomfortable they will become. While you might prefer to avoid feeling unpleasant emotions such as shame, anger, fear, and disappointment, pleasant and unpleasant emotions are like two sides to the same coin; you cannot avoid unpleasant emotions without limiting your ability to feel pleasant emotions such as joy, excitement, and delight.

Weather in the Sky

This activity can help you appreciate your emotions as a constantly changing phenomenon, like the weather. If you find it difficult to visualize things, you can complete this activity by drawing a picture or reading this activity aloud and considering what it means. You may benefit from stimming during this exercise to help you feel calm and keep your attention. If helpful, lie down, place a weighted blanket over yourself, or play background music. You will find a recording of this exercise at https://www.newharbinger.com/53073.

Take a moment to settle yourself in any position that feels comfortable for you. Close your eyes and take several long, slow, deep breaths.

Imagine the sky on a sunny day—calm and blue. Clouds are drifting by, some fragile and wispy, others thick and fluffy, and yet others are grey storm clouds, foreboding and full of rain. The weather is constantly changing. One day, you have a thunderstorm, winter blizzard, or swirling tornado, while there's nothing but fluffy white clouds on another day.

If you don't like the weather, you might try to control it. You shake your fist at the sky and tell the bad weather to stay away, but you cannot seem to make the storms disappear. So, you try to ignore it but to achieve this, you must go inside. Going inside will help you avoid the storms, but you'll also miss the sunny days. In the end, you realize that controlling the weather is impossible. It's just going to happen regardless of what you want.

Remember that no matter the weather, the blue sky is always there, even if you can't always see it. Imagine that you are the sky, and your emotions are the weather. The sky always has room for the weather, just as your mind and body always have room for your emotions, no matter what they are.

Notice any emotions inside you right now. Allow them to be there as if they are clouds drifting by. Even if you sometimes feel like you might be swept away by a storm, you know that eventually, the weather will pass, and the sky will still be there, calm, blue, and unchanged.

Bring this exercise to a close by taking a few long, slow, deep breaths. Allow the images to fade in their own time. Gently bring yourself back to your day.

Take a moment to reflect on your relationship with your emotions, then describe what might be possible if you could let your emotions come and go as if they were the weather and you were the sky.

_____

_____

_____

_____

_____

_____

Being willing to experience powerful emotions, whether pleasant or unpleasant, without fighting, suppressing, or running from them is the pathway to greater life satisfaction. Developing your ability to regulate these emotions will lead you to greater wellbeing and better mental health. Mastering these skills will take time and practice, but is worth it.

In the next chapter, you will explore how to stop being so unkind to yourself and how to get things done. Both will challenge your budding skills in emotion regulation, because they will expose you to self-criticism and possibly feelings of shame. Remember to treat yourself gently and take plenty of breaks to self-soothe using the PRIMA approach.

CHAPTER 5

Stop Beating Yourself Up and Get Things Done

Normal is not something to aspire to, it's something to get away from.

—Jodie Foster

Your house is a mess; dirty dishes, laundry, paperwork, and bills pile up. You miss appointments and always seem to be fixing problems you've caused by forgetting something. You have difficulty finishing your assignments, completing paperwork, and meeting work deadlines. You berate yourself by saying:

"Why do I waste so much time?"

"There's something wrong with me."

"I'm so lazy."

"Everyone else can do this—why can't I?"

Feeling like you are failing, you try to hide these problems as much as possible. Yet despite telling yourself off and trying your hardest, things keep going wrong. Other people only offer solutions that work best for them, such as "Use a diary," "Write a list," and "Try a bullet journal." Some of these strategies work for a while, but sooner or later, things fall apart again.

If you struggle to get things done, you are not alone. Getting organized and getting things done is an extremely common and frustrating problem for ADHDers and most Autistic people. By the time you reached adulthood, you may have received thousands of messages about not meeting other people's expectations. You keep being told, "You need to try harder," "Stop getting so distracted," "Concentrate on what you are doing," or "Stop messing around and just get on with it!" If only it were that simple. Unfortunately, our society consistently places the blame for this problem on the person who is stuck. You are expected to stop procrastinating, prioritize, stay focused, and be more self-disciplined despite these things not being easy for your neurodivergent brain, and without any meaningful help.

In this chapter, you'll learn how to let go of your habit of harshly criticizing yourself and harness the strengths of your spiky profile to get the important things in your life done. This will involve challenging unrealistic expectations and being more compassionate to yourself when you can't meet other people's ideals. We have many practical ideas and suggestions; however, we understand that this work can be a little over-whelming initially. For this reason, we recommend trying just one or two new strategies at a time. If something helps, great—keep doing it! Remember that there are no magic solutions. Any strategy that increases your likelihood of completing a task can be worth sticking with, even if it does not work 100 percent of the time. Getting things done more often is better than not at all, and there may be a way you can build on this success.

Why It's So Hard to Get Things Done

To achieve your goals and daily chores successfully, your approach must address the obstacles getting in your way. There can be so many factors contributing to your difficulty getting started and finishing things that it can be challenging to know why you are so stuck. The barriers you face are complex and may include several of the following:

- You are striving to meet unattainable, perfectionistic standards.

- You are trying to meet unrealistic neuronormative expectations.

- Your executive functioning is overloaded.

- The things you are trying to do are too boring or repetitive, or not challenging enough.

- You are trying to do everything yourself without any help.

- The strategies you are using don't suit your neurodivergent brain.

- Your body gets physically stuck, and you can't get it moving.

- You feel pressured, resistant, and resentful of the demands placed on you.

Each section that follows considers one of these barriers and explores how you can harness your neuro-divergent strengths to overcome it. But first, you'll need one particular self-compassion skill: being less judgmental of yourself.

It's Time to Stop Beating Yourself Up

You live in a world that often equates a person's worth with their productivity. Yet no matter what people have said or what you believe, *you are not lazy*. You've been working hard to keep everyone happy *and* achieve your goals, so laziness cannot be the problem (Price 2021).

Staying focused and on task is challenging for many neurodivergent people because it requires all aspects of executive functioning, particularly task initiation, switching focus, maintaining attention, organization, and impulse control. The kind of restless energy that distracts you with tiny details and overwhelms you with complexity could have been beneficial for your ancient ancestors. Back then, having members of the community who could quickly scan the environment for threats or search all day for food would have been extremely useful. Unfortunately, in modern society, this scattered attention makes it difficult to draft your thesis or consistently do the dishes.

It's time to give yourself a break from constant self-criticism and begin to view your thoughts with a bit of healthy skepticism. Humans are not always rational thinkers, and this applies to you too. Tens of thousands of thoughts go through your mind daily, and many are just pointless chatter or a dull narration of your daily activities. The usefulness of your thinking ranges from essential and groundbreaking to random worries and meaningless waffling.

In the following activities, you will look at your thoughts in two ways. First, you'll see what it is like to have greater distance from your self-critical thoughts. Next, you'll practice speaking to yourself more gently, with a warmer tone of voice. As you put the remaining strategies in this chapter into action, you'll have plenty of opportunities to practice both these skills.

Get Some Distance from Self-Critical Thoughts

Consider the observations and judgments you make of yourself and how they form an ongoing commentary that can be hurtful and mean. This inner dialogue may become critical and even nasty when you don't achieve your goals. Write down five hurtful things you say to yourself. These could be something like "I can never follow through on my plans," or "I am hopeless at being organized."

_____

_____

_____

_____

Consider how repeatedly saying these things to yourself affects how you feel. Circle any words below describing the emotions that come up when you criticize yourself, adding any others in the spaces provided.

Aggravated	Embarrassed	Lost
Annoyed	Frustrated	Unhappy
Ashamed	Grumpy	Upset
Depressed	Helpless	Worthless
Despairing	Hopeless	_____
Discouraged	Humiliated	_____
Disgusted	Irritable	_____

To explore how to get some distance from the self-critical statements you've written above, try the following simple activity.

Step 1: I'm Having the Thought

Read each self-critical statement aloud, adding the following phrase at the start: *"I'm having the thought that…"* For example, *"I'm having the thought that* I can never follow through on my plans" or *"I am having the thought that* I am hopeless at being organized." As you read each aloud with this added phrase, notice how the intensity of the statement might change.

Step 2: I'm Noticing That I'm Having the Thought

Read the statements aloud once again, but this time, add an extra phrase to the start: *"I'm noticing that* I am having the thought that…" For example, *"I'm noticing that I'm having the thought that* I can never follow through on my plans" or *"I'm noticing that I'm having the thought that* I am hopeless at being organized."

Briefly describe any further changes you notice to the intensity of your self-critical statements with this phrase added.

_____

_____

_____

What you say to yourself and how you say it matters. You cannot control your thoughts, but you can practice saying kinder, gentler, and more understanding things to yourself when you are struggling.

Offer Yourself Some Words of Kindness

In this activity, you will practice speaking to yourself using a warm and kind tone of voice. You can do this activity either sitting, lying, or standing. Do what feels most comfortable for you. You will find a recording of this exercise at https://www.newharbinger.com/53073.

Close your eyes or soften your focus, then take several slow, deep breaths. Begin to soften the tension in your body. With the next slow breath, soften your shoulders. With the next, soften your jaw. Then soften your forehead and behind your eyes. Let your limbs soften and relax. Let go of any points of tension in your body and allow it to slow down. If you begin to feel restless or fidgety at any time, allow yourself to wriggle or adjust your position, then return to settling your body as best you can.

When you are comfortable and calm, say the following statements aloud using a warm tone of voice. Take your time. Pause after each statement to absorb the kind intention behind the words.

May you be well.

May you be happy.

May you be free of suffering.

Now, repeat this process, but this time, say these statements aloud with an even warmer and kinder tone of voice. If you feel like you are acting, that's okay. Pause after each sentence to listen and absorb the feelings of warmth. If you become distracted by your thoughts, take a deep breath and put these thoughts aside.

Finally, say the statements aloud once more with as much warmth and kindness as you can. Put everything you have into this performance, while focusing on the kind intention behind the words. Allow a gentle smile to form on your face.

Take a few more deep breaths as you begin to bring this activity to a close. Acknowledge the effort you've made in completing this. Use three more deep breaths to absorb any lingering warm feelings before you return to your day.

Complete the following sentence to capture the sensations you noticed in your body as you said these warm, kind words to yourself. You may like to refer to the list of *Sensations Many People Feel in Their Bodies* in chapter 3 and the emotions listed in chapter 4 for ideas.

I noticed:

_____ in my _____, and

_____ in my _____, and

_____ in my _____.

Describe how you could practice this activity in your daily life.

_____

_____

_____

_____

Learning to be kinder to yourself is the first step toward being more productive and building greater long-term wellbeing. It may have felt awkward and unfamiliar to speak to yourself with kindness and warmth at first, but with repeated practice it can become easier. You may also like to follow this activity with a moment of self-care, such as one of the following:

- Rest or lie down with a weighted blanket

- Wrap yourself in something soft or soothing

- Get a hug from a trusted person or pet

- Make yourself a cup of tea or your favorite snack

- Gaze at a favorite object, image, or color

- Listen to a comforting sound or piece of music

- Just do nothing at all for a few minutes

If you find it hard to speak to yourself in a kinder way, do not give up. It will take time and practice to develop these skills. You may also find it easier to offer yourself more compassion once you examine the standards you set for yourself. You may find that you are holding yourself to ideals that are unrealistic and don't reflect what is important to you. Choosing your own priorities and setting realistic standards will give you much less reason to criticize yourself and is just one of many ways you can make your life easier.

Reevaluate Priorities and Let Go of Unattainable Ideals

Like many neurodivergent people, you may have high expectations of yourself. Your standards are likely to be higher than those that non-neurodivergent people have for themselves. Aiming to have everyone like you, deliver the highest quality work, get the highest grade, or have your home consistently tidy, organized, and efficient are unrealistic and perfectionistic expectations based on neuronormative ideals. Perfectionism is a problematic pattern not limited to stereotypical overachievers and can cause enormous stress and anxiety (Kemp 2021). *Unhelpful perfectionism* is when you:

- Set extremely ambitious and inflexible standards for yourself and tend to raise these standards each time you achieve them

- Are intensely afraid of failure and mistakes, including making social mistakes and other people not liking you

- Experience persistent, demoralizing self-criticism and never feel good enough because you can't meet your standards for success

- Tend to avoid situations where you might fail or make a mistake, including situations where other people might judge you, and then experience problems in your life because of this avoidance

Unfortunately, standards that demand flawless performance are impossible to meet and leave you feeling like a failure (Kemp 2021). Fear of potential failure will ignite your threat system, making you feel anxious, under constant threat, and on the edge of exhaustion. The extra burden on your executive functioning makes it more difficult to solve problems, prioritize, get organized, and make decisions. Perfectionism can also activate your drive system, keeping you striving to meet unattainable ideals even if you are not succeeding.

How often do you hold yourself to standards that are extremely difficult to achieve?

Circle one:

Never   Rarely   Sometimes   Often   Very Often   Always

How often do you raise the standards you set for yourself after you've achieved a goal?

Circle one:

Never   Rarely   Sometimes   Often   Very Often   Always

It is valid and acceptable to arrange your life in a way that works best for you. Household chores aren't inherently good or bad—in fact, they have no moral value at all. Not doing them doesn't make you less worthy as a person (Davis 2022). Some simple ways you can challenge neuronormative expectations in your home life and make things easier for yourself are as follows:

- Wear the same outfit each day, choose from just a limited number of clothes, or only wear clothes in your favorite color.

- Sort your laundry into several baskets. Keep your clothes in these baskets rather than folding and putting them away. Put all dirty clothes in another basket ready for washing.

- Don't iron anything, ever. There are plenty of beautiful and comfortable clothes in fabrics that don't need ironing.

- Simplify cooking by eating the same thing each day, preparing one big meal to eat during the week, or buying meal kits.

- Avoid cooking altogether by using a meal delivery service or buying ready-made meals.

By challenging neuronormative expectations, you can create simple systems that lighten the load on your executive functioning. Reducing this burden frees up your capacity for other tasks.

Reduce the Burden on Your Executive Functioning

You have a finite amount of mental energy and focus, and there is always competition for these limited resources. Given how sensitive and hyperconnected neurodivergent nervous systems can be, the mental resources you need to get things done must be shared with other mental functions, such as processing sensory experiences, noticing tiny details, and staying focused. These use up your ability to focus, which explains why it can be more difficult to concentrate and think clearly if your clothes are too scratchy, it's too hot, or everyone is talking at once. As a neurodivergent person once told me, "I can't think properly when I'm wearing shoes."

Spoon theory is a metaphor developed by Christine Miserandino in 2003 that is often used in the context of chronic illness or disability. This metaphor represents your limited energy and mental capacity each day as spoons (Miserandino 2003). Each task you complete during the day uses a certain number of spoons, but you usually don't have enough spoons to allow you to do everything you'd like to do. When you run out of spoons, you feel overwhelmed and exhausted—and unable to do anything further until you replace your spoons through rest and recovery.

How often do you feel overwhelmed like you have run out of spoons?

Circle one:

Never   Rarely   Sometimes   Often   Very Often   Always

Spoon theory is helpful when considering how every task you are juggling adds to the burden on your executive functioning. One way you can protect yourself from becoming overburdened is to reduce the number of mental spoons you need by simplifying and restructuring daily tasks. Conserving your spoons is an act of self-compassion.

Restructure and Simplify Tasks

To reduce your organizational burden, the best place to start is exploring how to simplify your choices and create simple routines by grouping tasks together. For instance, you can:

- Put the thing you often forget with something you never forget, such as your shopping list on top of your car keys or medications inside your empty coffee cup.

- Link tasks together, such as brushing your teeth while in the shower.

- Pair tasks with something already in your routine, such as drinking a glass of water whenever you wash your hands.

- Create a drop zone by your front door where you place everything you will need when you leave the house.

Use Technology to Support You

A key strategy that can simplify your life is outsourcing as much as possible. Fortunately, there are many ways you can use technology to supplement your executive functions of organizing, prioritizing, and remembering things, such as:

- Set alarms to remind you to complete specific tasks like managing your medications, drinking water, playing relaxing music at bedtime, or completing your nighttime routine. Keep snoozing the alarm until you get it done.

- Use a habit tracker app to measure your progress and habit streaks.

- Put *everything* into a single online calendar, even obvious things. Have this calendar accessible on your phone. You may consider investing in a smartwatch that can link to your calendar.

- Set timers to remind you to do something later, such as check the oven, turn off the hose, or get ready to go out. Alternatively, schedule a text to your own phone or use home-based technology such as Google or Alexa by saying, "Remind me to remove the laundry from the washing machine in one hour."

Ask Artificial Intelligence to Solve Problems

The applications of technology and artificial intelligence (AI) are expanding every day. You can use AI to solve problems, develop ideas, make decisions, get organized, and get things done. AI can help you:

- Break complex problems into a simple plan that considers your specific needs and creates a realistic schedule, which could also be in a theme related to your spin.

- Set priorities when you are juggling multiple demands.

- Develop a plan to achieve a desired outcome, such as getting your dream job.

- Create a study schedule that is adapted to your learning preferences.

- Create an exercise plan sensitive to your physical and mental health needs.

- Create a grocery list and meal plan based on your intolerances or dietary requirements, health conditions, and budget.

- Provide options for fun or entertaining activities, such as what to do with the kids on a rainy day.

- Generate ideas about how to make boring tasks more novel or fun.

- Help you start an assignment or report by giving you an example of how to structure your argument.

- Draft emails with a specific tone of voice, such as lighthearted, professional, or approachable.

- Tell you what to write on a greeting card.

Stop Doing Everything Yourself

Humans have always helped each other and collaborated to solve problems; our ancestors would not have survived without working together. Even in our complex modern world, no one can be good at everything. To be successful, we need to help each other. Asking for help is a self-compassionate action; however, as a neurodivergent person, even when you want help it can be difficult to ask. You may have a history of rejection that makes asking feel unsafe or painful. It's vital to overcome this barrier because asking others for help will make many things more accessible for you. In chapter 8, you will have further opportunities to explore how to advocate for yourself.

How often do you ask others for help?

Circle one:

Never   Rarely   Sometimes   Often   Very Often   Always

Given how uncomfortable seeking help can be, be gentle with yourself as you begin. Start by asking people you trust for help in small ways. If finances permit or funding is available, accessing paid support could also help because it feels less personal and rejection isn't an issue. Here are some kinds of paid help you could seek out:

- Housekeeping services to help with cleaning, preparing food, or gardening.

- A decluttering coach or disability worker to help with organizing your home.

- A laborer or handyman to help with physical jobs around the home.

- A virtual assistant or bookkeeper to keep everything on track, particularly if you have your own business and struggle to keep up with paperwork and bills.

There are no prizes for doing everything on your own. Whether you ask trusted friends, pay for services from others, or use technology, you can find support to help you get your jobs done.

Harness Your Neurodivergent Strengths for Greater Efficiency

A range of strategies are available that harness your neurodivergent spiky profile in ways that can help you overcome problems with boredom, getting started, persisting at uninteresting tasks, and finishing things efficiently. Let's look at strategies that make the most of your strengths.

Overcome Boredom by Making Things NICE

ADHDers and many Autistic people find boredom painful and distressing. Your brain is oriented toward the things you find interesting, whether they are long-term monotropic interests or short-term intense hyperfixations. You will be naturally drawn to activities that are Novel, Interesting, Challenging, or (an) Emergency (or NICE).

Some of the qualities that make a task NICE are listed below. Place a checkmark next to those you find enjoyable and satisfying.

☐ Solving difficult or complex problems

☐ Finding the most efficient way to do things

☐ Beating a record, gaining a high score, or winning a competition

☐ Doing things as fast as possible

☐ Innovating to create something new

☐ Making something aesthetically pleasing

☐ Adding new items to your collection

☐ Making a discovery

☐ Deepening your knowledge and understanding

☐ Discovering how something works

☐ Making sense of complex information

☐ Solving puzzles

☐ Other: _____

By giving activities NICE qualities you can harness your strengths and stay focused much more easily. You may even become so engrossed that you lose track of time.

Unfortunately, when presented with a task that does not have NICE qualities, it can feel as if your brain slams down the shutters and shouts a loud and undeniable "No!" When this happens, a task may need to become an emergency to give you enough activating adrenaline to get it done.

How often do you leave things until the last minute so they become an emergency?

Circle one:

Never   Rarely   Sometimes   Often   Very Often   Always

You can harness your preference for NICE tasks by finding ways to make boring tasks more interesting and engaging. If this is not possible, you may need to create urgency to activate your emergency response. Here are some ideas for you to try:

- Create a problem you can solve.

- Find the most efficient way of doing something or setting up a new system.

- "Gamify" chores using an app and collect points or rewards. There are many apps available and designed different purposes, such as Habitica for chores, Forest for productivity and focus, Dry Days for quitting unhealthy habits, Plant Nanny for drinking water, and Finch for mental health.

- Create competition by setting yourself a target to beat or racing a friend.

- Create urgency by giving yourself a deadline to complete the activity.

- Find creative and unusual ways to complete the task.

- Find ways to make the task more beautiful or symmetrical.

- Link the task to one of your other interests, such as the theme of your favorite movie or animated character.

Use the Power of Body Doubling

Sometimes, boring jobs still need to get done. For these, it is useful to ask a friend or family member for assistance. One of the best ways they can help you is through body doubling. Body doubling means having someone help you get started and work alongside you, making it easier to get the task done. It is an effective strategy people were using long before the term existed. Your body double can be a friend or close family member who helps you with work, study, or hobbies. They might be physically with you, online, or on the phone, doing their own work, supporting you with your work, being completely quiet, or offering occasional encouragement.

How often do you use body doubling to get things done?

Circle one:

Never   Rarely   Sometimes   Often   Very Often   Always

Briefly describe the kinds of activities where body doubling could help you stay focused and achieve more. These could be enjoyable hobbies, work, or study.

_____

_____

_____

_____

List up to six people you could ask to be your body double.

_____   _____

_____   _____

_____   _____

Stay Focused by Optimizing Your Level of Stimulation

Boredom feels uncomfortable for anyone, but can be excruciating for ADHDers. If you tend to need a lot of stimulation to stay focused, you may need to increase your sensory input to stay on task. Here are some ways you can achieve this:

- Have multiple channels of information on while you work, such as videos, gaming, podcasts, or your favorite TV shows.

- Access the same information through multiple sources simultaneously, such as listening to an audiobook while reading the pages or watching lectures while reading the transcript.

- Say each step of what you are doing aloud as you complete it. This will keep the task in your working memory and help you stay focused.

- Listen to lectures or e-books while walking or driving, or work on your hobby while attending meetings.

- Take notes of key points or draw diagrams to stay actively engaged when learning.

- Use stimming strategies to keep yourself activated.

Use Hyperfocus to Get Things Done Efficiently

If you listen to your body's rhythms and energy levels, you can use hyperfocus to work hard when you can, and rest when you need to. Here are some ways that you can harness hyperfocus mode:

- Aim to get as much as possible done during a limited time, such as giving yourself fifteen minutes to tidy the living room.

- Cluster together similar activities and complete them in a ten-minute surge of hyper-productivity, such as opening and sorting all your mail or making three phone calls.

- Create a daily "sprint" that makes life easier for "future you," such as spending five minutes tidying up the kitchen or putting tomorrow's clothes out before you go to bed.

You can always extend any of these tasks to keep your hyperfocus going longer, but remember to eat, drink water, go to the toilet, and stop before you burn out.

Get Yourself Unstuck and Moving

Sometimes, no matter how much you want or need to do something, you can't seem to get your body to do it. People in the field have only recently begun calling this problem *Autistic inertia* or *ADHD paralysis*. Inside, you may feel restless, agitated, and frustrated, but there is a disconnect between your intentions and actions, and you cannot move (Buckle et al. 2021).

Inertia is not consistent. It tends to come and go. You may have difficulty getting going, have difficulty stopping once you have started, or struggle to switch between tasks. At times, you may feel productive and capable, while at other times, you only realize that you have been stuck when someone or something disrupts you.

How often do you experience this kind of physical inertia?

Circle one:

Never   Rarely   Sometimes   Often   Very Often   Always

Briefly describe an experience where you got stuck and what eventually got you moving.

_____

_____

_____

_____

Activating your body gradually through movement may help you get started and stay focused longer. Look for fun, interesting things you can do with your body. Here are some ideas:

- Gradually increase your activation by stimming. Do whatever feels easy and fun.

- Listen to music and allow your body to move with the rhythm.

- Take movement breaks during the day, using these as opportunities to keep your body active.

- Take a walk, swim, ride a bike, run, or do any other exercise. Exercising in the morning may help you focus during the day.

- Ask a friend or family member to gently remind you to get started.

We don't know the causes of Autistic inertia and ADHD paralysis. Hopefully, researchers will have some answers soon. In the meantime, it's okay to ask the people around you to gently nudge you into action.

Approach Demands with Flexibility

Elizabeth Newson coined the term *pathological demand avoidance* in the 1980s, defining it as "extreme resistance to the ordinary demands of life." Some people consider pathological demand avoidance to be a specific profile of Autism, while others see it as a separate neurotype altogether (Hess 2022; O'Nions et al. 2021). There is debate about the most descriptive and affirming way to describe this phenomenon, with alternatives including "extreme demand avoidance" or "pervasive drive for autonomy." For simplicity, we use "demand avoidance."

Demand avoidance is a powerful, distressing, and overwhelming feeling that surges whenever you feel overburdened by the expectations of other people or yourself. The demands on you feel so instantly and overwhelmingly anxiety-provoking that you must immediately reject them and may react angrily or become upset. The things you experience as demands are not limited to requests like washing the dishes or tidying up; they can include anything that uses your energy or attention, or has sensory, social, or emotional implications for you (Egan, Linenberg, and O'Nions 2019).

People who experience demand avoidance seem to have a threat system that is extremely sensitive to demands and expectations. Anything outside your control has the potential to trigger the sympathetic nervous system into fight-or-flight mode, resulting in overwhelming anxiety, anger, and defensiveness. It's no wonder many people who experience demand avoidance have a higher need for autonomy (O'Nions et al. 2021).

The biggest challenge for me is feeling boxed in and confined by all the things expected of me. Whenever I'm in structured environments like school and university, I feel restricted and controlled—and a strong urge to resist that paralyzes me with shame. Only when the due date gets closer and it becomes more painful can I finally break free, switch into hyperfocus, and work frantically for hours. It hasn't always been enough to get good grades, but I've managed to scrape through. Nowadays, I work to my own timelines as much as I can. —Grant

To understand how problematic and intense your experience of demand avoidance is, complete the following questions by checking all that apply.

Do you sometimes or often:

- ☐ Tend to get angry very quickly if someone makes an unexpected or unwanted request

- ☐ Prefer to be in control rather than follow others

- ☐ Feel a strong urge to resist expectations placed on you

- ☐ Have difficulty following orders given by authority figures

- ☐ Feel reluctant to do things unless you have a good understanding of what is required

- ☐ Feel very strongly that other people should follow the rules, but do not always feel those rules should apply to you

☐ Tend to argue with rules if you feel they are arbitrary or meaningless

☐ Use shocking or confrontational behavior to avoid doing something

☐ Avoid doing things even when there may be negative consequences for you

If you checked many of these items, demand avoidance may pose a significant challenge for you. It may interfere with achieving your goals, affect your mood, and leave you and others feeling frustrated. If you have quite intense demand avoidance, you may prefer to resist society's expectations and live outside normal social roles. You may have also found traditional schooling and workplace demands too constraining, preferring to work for yourself or in your own way. If you find that others do not share your views on rules, hierarchy, and compliance, it may contribute to conflict and isolation.

Demand avoidance can be particularly challenging to manage when it is triggered by the expectations you have of yourself. It may worsen during burnout when you are already overloaded or when you have unrealistic expectations of yourself. If you can make your life more comfortable and ease your burnout, your demand avoidance may lower too, making tasks easier to complete and less distressing. It may also help if you can identify the origins of your demand-avoidant response and develop ways to overcome these issues.

Overcoming Your Demand Avoidance

This activity follows a four-step process to help you understand and manage your demand avoidance. You can download this activity as a worksheet at https://www.newharbinger.com/53073.

Step 1: Understanding Your Needs and Reactions

Complete the table below by describing a task that triggers demand avoidance. We've included an example to illustrate the process.

Question	Example Situation	Your Situation
The expectation, request, or demand that makes you feel upset	*I have to pack away all my hobbies and craft materials every time my in-laws come over.*	
Who asks you to do it	*My partner.*	

Question	Example Situation	Your Situation
How you feel about doing it	*Frustrated and resentful that I must do this every time.*	
Your reasons why you don't want to do the task	*It takes ages to pack things up and unpack them later. If I don't have the energy to do this, I can't spend time on my hobbies.*	
Your reactions and urges when asked	*I get grumpy and frustrated. I want to refuse to do it at all.*	
How your reaction fits with how you want to treat others	*I love my partner; I want to treat them respectfully and always be kind.*	
How you would prefer to respond	*I would like to stay calm and be able to do this easily.*	

Part 2: Consider Other Perspectives

Now, consider alternative ways of viewing this request from the perspective of the person asking. If you are writing about a demand you place on yourself, consider why the task is important to you and what outcome you want.

Question	Example Situation	Your Situation
Why the task is important to the person asking	*They want the house clean and tidy because their parents can be judgmental. Being tidy helps them relax.*	

Question	Example Situation	Your Situation
The outcome they want to achieve	*They don't want to be criticized by their parents. I know this is very painful for them.*	
How they feel when you react this way	*They get upset with me and look very hurt.*	
How my reaction causes problems or makes things worse	*When I get angry, my partner doesn't want to spend time with me. We might argue right before their parents arrive, which is stressful.*	

Part 3: Identify Your Barriers

There can be many barriers to completing a task. Consider what makes this particular task frustrating or difficult for you to complete. Check any items below that reflect your experience and add any others in the space provided.

Is the task:

☐ Too complex, confusing, or unclear?

☐ Not aligned with your interests, hyperfixations, or spins?

☐ Not interesting, enjoyably challenging, or urgent?

☐ Adding to your to-do list when you are already feeling overwhelmed?

☐ Disrupting you when you are doing other things?

☐ Going to be uncomfortable due to sensory stressors?

☐ Making you feel anxious, uneasy, or uncertain?

☐ Too physically exhausting or time-consuming?

☐ Not the best way of achieving the outcome?

☐ An unrealistic, neuronormative expectation?

☐ Being asked in a way that feels overly demanding, angry, or resentful toward you?

☐ Other: _____

Addressing these barriers is the key to being able to complete the task. Using the information above, describe up to three reasons why you feel upset or overburdened when asked to do this task.

1. _____

2. _____

3. _____

Part 4: Find Creative Ways to Address the Barriers

Consider how you can address the barriers you've identified above by making the task more comfortable and easier for you. Complete the final part of this activity by generating as many creative solutions as possible to address these barriers. You can choose to complete all the questions or only those that are relevant, based on your answers above.

Questions	Example Situation	Your Situation
How Could You:		
Make the task simpler?	I could ask my partner to help me set up a storage system that makes it easier to pack and unpack.	
Align the task to your hyperfixations or spins?	I enjoy organizing my materials. Having labeled boxes will make tidying up easier and more satisfying.	
Make it more interesting, enjoyably challenging, or urgent?	Creating a satisfying, elegant organizational system would be an enjoyable challenge.	

Questions	Example Situation	Your Situation
Reduce the complexity or size of effort required?	*It would make things simpler if everything had a place it belonged. I can also ask others for help.*	
Make it easier to switch your focus from other things?	*I can ask my partner to remind me that their parents are coming one hour before they are due to arrive.*	
Address the sensory discomfort associated with the task?	*Having things in attractive boxes would look nice and feel less messy and confusing.*	
Feel more confident and certain about doing the task?	*I can ask my friend Sarah to help me. She is good at organizing things.*	
Make the task less physically exhausting?	*I can use boxes that aren't too big or heavy, and put them where they are easy to reach.*	
Define a better way of solving the problem?	*I could set up a bench in the shed for craft.*	
Redefine the expectation to be realistic and not neuronormative?	*Unfortunately, my in-laws do have unreasonable expectations. I will support my partner in talking to them if they want to do this.*	
Get people to ask you in a way that feels less demanding?	*Ask my partner to say, "Could we tidy up your craft materials when you have finished what you are doing?"*	

Questions	Example Situation	Your Situation
Any other ways you could make the task easier to complete:	*Ask my partner to body double me while I tidy up.*	

Now that you've considered the alternatives, how willing are you to complete the task? Place an X on the line to reflect your current degree of willingness to complete the task.

I am more willing to do the task.   I am less willing to do the task.

•——•

If you wish to extend your understanding of demand avoidance, search for content by neurodivergent people on TikTok, YouTube, or your preferred video streaming platform. Make a note of any key points that resonate with your experience.

_____

_____

_____

It can be difficult to create a lifestyle that balances the expectations of adulthood with your need for freedom, choice, and autonomy. Having a better understanding of your demand avoidance can give you a better ability to manage your reactions, achieve your goals, and support healthy relationships.

Discuss Medications with Your Doctor

Despite the stigma attached to stimulant medications, many ADHDers find that the right medication is life-changing. When you are on the right medication, task initiation can become easier, you may think more clearly, and you may be less overwhelmed by complexity and uncertainty. The right medication will support your memory, attention, and focus and help you juggle competing priorities.

Medications do not work for some people, while others find that they become so productive they can overdo it and burn out. To explore the possibility of medications, you will need to find a trusted and affirming doctor who will check your overall health and compatibility with any other medications you might be taking. Only ever use medications under medical supervision.

If Nothing Else, Do Just One Thing

In this chapter, you've been given a wide range of strategies that can get you started—so many that it might seem a bit daunting. Take this opportunity to narrow down your focus by completing the following prompts.

One strategy that you will try straight away: _____

Three strategies that could be helpful, and you'll try as soon as you can:

1. _____

2. _____

3. _____

Three longer-term changes that you'd like to make:

1. _____

2. _____

3. _____

Remember that no matter what strategies you use, it's important to pace yourself. Doing too much too quickly can lead to burnout. If you feel overwhelmed, remember that doing nothing is valid too. Sometimes, you need to rest and recharge. As you begin working toward your goals, remember to start small, avoid setting unrealistic expectations for yourself, and consider having a simple focus of doing just one thing per day.

CHAPTER 6

Developing Safe, Supportive Relationships

Normal is not something to aspire to, it's something to get away from.

—Jodie Foster

Two of the most harmful stereotypes about neurodivergent people are that (1) we do not want human connections and that (2) we cannot relate to others—but this is not the case. Neurodivergent people need social connections as much as anyone else; however, the form these connections take often looks different. Given the high rates of trauma experienced by neurodivergent people, relationships need to feel safe to be enjoyable. If you have a lot of social connections but feel unsafe with most of those people, your threat system will be frequently activated and you will always feel on edge with them.

This chapter offers a gentle pathway that can take you from feeling isolated, anxious, and uneasy in relationships to feeling safer and more supported. You'll explore the barriers to making friends and identify practical strategies for developing safe connections. It can take months or years to build relationships (although there are some shortcuts you can take); the strategies you learn here will get you started in the right direction and improve your chances of success.

The topic of friendships can bring painful memories and grief to the surface, so please be particularly gentle with yourself as you work through this chapter. Part of this journey is learning to be a good friend to yourself too.

Why Relationships Can Be So Painful

For years, neurodivergent people have been told that they have deficits in social skills, yet the truth is that Autistic people and ADHDers simply connect with others in ways that are different from non-neurodivergent people—and are equally valid. Nevertheless, if you struggle with building friendships, it is worth exploring where and why your current approach isn't working. Your difficulties may come from spending time with people who don't understand you or perhaps you struggle to understand how others feel about you. You may also be trying to make friends by following neuronormative social rules that feel confusing and illogical to you.

Who you choose to spend time with is crucial to your experience of friendships. If you feel like your non-neurodivergent friends do not "get you," you could be right! Nonautistic people often have difficulty understanding and interpreting Autistic people's behavior, emotional states, and social cues (Edey et al. 2016; Sheppard et al. 2016). This may be one reason why communication difficulties between neurodivergent and non-neurodivergent people are so common. Being around people who do not understand you is emotionally draining, particularly if you feel you must constantly perform a version of yourself that they will accept.

How often do you feel like your friends "get you"?

Circle one:

Never   Rarely   Sometimes   Often   Very Often   Always

Relationships can be anxiety-provoking if you aren't sure how others feel about you, leading you to feel uneasy even with your friends. You may also spend a lot of time working out how other people feel, ruminating over conversations you've had, and attempting to decipher people's intentions from clues in their behavior. These patterns contribute to social anxiety, a challenge that approximately half of Autistic and ADHDer adults face (Maddox and White 2015).

Place an X on the line to reflect how anxious you feel in social situations.

I feel very anxious and uncertain   I feel calm, confident, and
in social situations.   relaxed in social situations.

●——●

Social situations will feel draining and confusing if you are trying to make friendships by following social rules that feel illogical or inconsistent to you. You will inevitably make some small social mistake, adding to your anxiety. Socializing in neuronormative ways, such as going out in big groups, going to busy restaurants, or attending concerts, matches, or shows involves extensive exposure to sensory stressors including noises, bright lights, and lots of people. Choosing what you want to eat, managing your food preferences in public, and tracking conversations in noisy environments or where many people are talking at once can quickly overwhelm your executive functioning. While the event may initially be exciting, your energy may be hard to sustain. It's impossible to give your best social performance when you are heading for a meltdown or shutdown. You may eventually become irritable or be unable to speak and feel completely burned-out afterward.

Given how painful relationships can be, it is understandable that you might consider giving up on making friends altogether. The urge to withdraw comes from a deep need for safety, but not having any close connections leaves you in a lonely place where you do not feel important or valued by others. Being disconnected from meaningful relationships is linked to depression. And unfortunately, the more you isolate yourself, the more socially anxious you will become.

Let's pause for a moment.

Notice how you are feeling right now as you think about friendships. This may be similar to how you feel in social situations. If you feel anxious, agitated, hopeless, detached, or empty, your threat system may have been activated. If so, take some time right now to regulate your emotions and self-soothe. While you might feel tempted to plow ahead and ignore how uncomfortable and vulnerable you feel, this is a chance to practice the PRIMA approach to activate your soothing system. Care for yourself compassionately by using soothing rhythm breathing, stimming, or connecting with your interests. Reach out for support if needed. As you begin to feel calmer and more in control, consider what these emotions tell you about your experience of friendships and how you feel about them now. Then, when you are ready, read on to explore how to build safe, supportive connections in a gentle and self-compassionate way.

Transforming Rejection to Connection

Developing social connections with people who appreciate you for who you are is possible. However, to successfully create these supportive relationships, you may need a radically different approach from what you are doing now. Creating supportive and safe relationships depends on five elements:

1. Building relationships on a foundation of self-compassion

2. Connecting in a way that feels authentic to you

3. Finding people who share your neurotype—your *neurokin*

4. Nurturing friendships with a small number of people who get you

5. Letting go of trying to keep everyone happy

At first, this might feel daunting. As you may have noticed, even thinking about friendships can trigger sensitivity to rejection and uncomfortable emotions. So, it's essential that you be very gentle and kind toward yourself at each step of this process. Remember to pause and self-regulate whenever needed along the way.

Build Relationships on a Foundation of Self-Compassion

It can be challenging to offer yourself kindness when you have a long history of painful experiences with others. You learn about yourself from your interactions with others, and over your lifetime, painful and hurtful feedback can develop into stories about yourself that you believe to be true. If you've blamed yourself for your difficulty establishing safe relationships or for hurtful experiences you've had in the past, you may tell yourself that people won't like you. Designed to keep you safe, this story has you preparing for rejection long before it happens—but it undermines your confidence too.

Place an X on the line to reflect your assumptions about how people feel about you.

I assume most people will dislike me.   I assume most people like me.

You may have gained other painful beliefs from past experiences or what others have said. Place a checkmark next to any of the following "self-stories" that feel true about you:

☐ I am always upsetting people.

☐ I am annoying.

☐ I am socially awkward.

☐ I am weird.

☐ I am unable to make friends.

☐ It is my fault when friendships break down.

☐ I am not liked by others unless I _____.

☐ I am always letting people down.

☐ Other: _____

Despite how certain you might feel that these stories are true, it is helpful to hold these stories lightly—which means realizing that they could be wrong. All the stories you have about yourself have the potential to become "word prisons" that limit what you can do (Twohig, Levin, and Ong 2021). Even the positive self-story "I am a loyal friend" could lead you to follow a friend's wishes in ways that don't fit your values. For this reason, it's not advisable to believe the stories you have about yourself without question.

Letting Go of Unhelpful Self-Stories

This activity helps you explore what it means to hold your self-stories lightly using "I am…" thoughts (Kemp 2021; Sandoz and DuFrene 2013). In the space below, write up to six stories you have about your ability to make and keep friendships. Start each statement with "I am…" These stories may be positively phrased, such as, "I am a loyal friend" or "I am generous," or be negative, like those listed above.

1. I am _____.

2. I am _____.

3. I am _____.

4. I am _____.

5. I am _____.

6. I am _____.

Look over what you've written and place an * next to the statements you feel most attached to—the stories you would defend as true, even if they aren't kind or flattering.

Now, let's do an experiment. Take a deep breath, then slowly strike out statement number 3 on your list. As you draw a line through this statement, imagine that this is no longer true of you. *Let it go.* Watch what happens inside yourself as you do this. Depending on what this statement said, it might feel upsetting, strange, unsettling, or a relief to let it go. If this is a strongly held belief, you may want to resist letting this go. Notice this too.

Next, do the same thing with number 5. Once again, as you strike it out, imagine that this is no longer true of you. *Let it go, too.* Notice what this feels like. Finally, strike out all the remaining items, one by one. With each, pause to notice how it feels to let the story go.

Describe up to three emotions and physical sensations you noticed as you struck out each statement and imagined it no longer applied to you. You may like to refer to the emotions listed in chapter 4 and the list of *Sensations Many People Feel in Their Bodies* in chapter 3.

Emotion: _____ Physical sensation: _____

Emotion: _____ Physical sensation: _____

Emotion: _____ Physical sensation: _____

Briefly describe what might be possible for you if you no longer believed these statements.

_____

_____

_____

Holding your self-stories lightly, as something that may or may not be true, allows you to develop a more flexible perspective on yourself and choose how you respond to situations in flexible ways.

Initiating new friendships takes courage. Given how tender and bruised you may feel from past friendships, it is understandable that you would feel wary of risking the pain of rejection. It will help if you can offer yourself support and compassion, even if being kinder to yourself feels strange and unfamiliar. Fortunately, simply imagining being with someone safe and supportive can help ease your distress at times of struggle (Steindl 2020). One strategy that can help you learn how to offer yourself greater understanding and kindness is creating a *Compassionate Other*.

Becoming a Supportive Friend to Yourself

Your Compassionate Other is an imaginary ally with whom you feel supported, cared for, and accepted. To connect with this compassionate extension of yourself, describe the personal qualities your Compassionate Other would embody, such as being *warm, caring, calm, kind, forgiving, patient, gentle,* and *understanding.* You can find further examples of personal qualities in chapter 7, in the list of *Personal Qualities That People Value.* Write the qualities you'd most like your Compassionate Other to have below.

_____

_____

_____

Consider how your Compassionate Other might look. For example, it could look like:

- A fictional character or superhero who is kind and cares deeply for others

- An imagined, ideal person, such as a gentle, loving, and wise older person

- A person who has been consistently kind toward you in the past

- A pet you loved as a child or that you still love as part of your family now

- A beautiful plant, animal, object, or physical environment

- A spiritual being that offers love and acceptance

Briefly describe the physical appearance of your Compassionate Other.

_____

_____

_____

You may like to draw a picture of your Compassionate Other in the space provided.

Compete the following visualization exercise to connect with what this ally can offer you. You will find an audio recording of this activity at https://www.newharbinger.com/53073.

> *Settle yourself into your chair in whatever way you feel comfortable: feet on the floor or your legs tucked up, crossed, or stretched out. Practice soothing rhythm breathing for several minutes, allowing your breathing to settle into a slow, steady rhythm while using any stimming that feels comforting. Consider moving*

your body gently by rocking from side to side, tapping your fingers, squeezing your hands, playing with your favorite fidget toy, stroking a textured item, or patting your pet…in other words, stim in any way that helps you to feel calm and focused.

Imagine that your Compassionate Other is sitting or standing by your side. You know they understand, accept you for who you are, and are willing to help. Imagine a sense of warmth and kindness flowing from your Compassionate Other to you.

Take a few slow, deep breaths as you notice what it feels like to receive compassion without judgment or criticism. Notice any reactions in your body. Appreciate what your Compassionate Other offers you for as long as you like.

Take a few more deep breaths, then, as you bring this activity to a close, acknowledge the presence of your Compassionate Other and the effort you have made to connect with this part of yourself. Then, when you are ready, open your eyes, move your body, and stretch.

Describe any emotions and physical sensations you experienced when you connected with your Compassionate Other.

Emotion: _____ Physical sensation: _____

Emotion: _____ Physical sensation: _____

Emotion: _____ Physical sensation: _____

Your Compassionate Other can provide soothing, nurturing, kindness, and connection while you work on developing safe, nurturing relationships with others. It may take some practice to receive this compassion if you are unfamiliar with receiving kindness from others. Connecting with compassion may also ignite feelings of grief and memories of hurtful experiences at first. If this happens, pause to regulate your emotions and care for yourself.

Connect in a Way That Feels Authentic

Neurodivergent people have different ways of connecting due to having different social preferences, communication styles, and values. Your social expectations and needs may differ fundamentally from those of the non-neurodivergent people you know. On the following pages, you will find descriptions of some of the most valued and enjoyed features of Autistic and ADHDer culture, including sharing your interests, going into detail and depth in conversations, giving thoughtful gifts, parallel play, exchanging stories, and having fast-paced, looping conversations. Neurodivergent connection also accepts silence. As you explore each social preference outlined below, find those that reflect your authentic preferences and give you the most joy, and complete the sentences to document your learning.

SHARING YOUR INTERESTS

Neurodivergent socializing often revolves around sharing through spins and hyperfixations. Whether you play games, role-play, cosplay, create art, cook, read books, or play sports, sharing these interests with others is often more fun. Engaging in your spin or hyperfixation energizes and regulates you, so socializing in ways that align with your interests can also help prevent burnout.

The spins or hyperfixations I particularly enjoy sharing with friends are _____

_____.

The people with whom I enjoy sharing this are _____

_____.

DIVING INTO DETAIL

Sharing knowledge and detailed understanding, often known as "info-dumping," is an accepted and appreciated part of Autistic and ADHDer culture. Taking turns to share details related to your favorite topics is something many neurodivergent people enjoy doing with people they like. Sharing what you have learned is a way of connecting; you hope what you share will be interesting, helpful, or exciting to the other person.

The detailed knowledge I particularly enjoy sharing with friends relates to my interests in

_____.

The people with whom I enjoy sharing this are _____

_____.

GIVING SMALL TOKENS THAT SHOW YOU CARE

Autistic people and ADHDers often enjoy giving gifts that they feel will be valued by the other person. This is called *penguin pebbling* after the way Gentoo penguin couples give each other pebbles to look after as they wait to lay their eggs. The pebbles become symbols of their shared relationship and commitment. A "pebble" could be anything you feel the other person would appreciate, such as a meme, TikTok video, rock, feather, leaf, book, or research article. Sharing this shows that you have thought about the person, care for them, and want to give them a small token that you know they will appreciate.

The kinds of penguin pebbles I enjoy sharing include _____

_____.

The people with whom I enjoy sharing penguin pebbles are _____

_____.

PLAYING IN PARALLEL

Often described as something Autistic children do, you engage in *parallel play* whenever you are with a friend yet enjoying separate activities. You could be working on separate craft projects, reading books, playing different games, or watching shows on your devices. A form of body doubling, parallel play can keep you focused. As it involves less back-and-forth conversation and direct eye contact, parallel play is a less demanding way to socialize. Parallel play is not just fun, it doesn't drain your "social battery" as fast.

The kinds of activities I enjoy doing in parallel play with friends are _____

_____.

The people with whom I enjoy parallel play are _____

_____.

EXCHANGING STORIES AND ANECDOTES

Autistic and ADHDer socializing often involves sharing anecdotes that demonstrate understanding and empathy. Sometimes reflecting the need to share before you forget what you are going to say, jumping in to share your story is accepted between Autistic people and ADHDers. The content of personal anecdotes could be anything; it will depend on the topic you are discussing with your friend. If you prefer to share deeply rather than engage in small talk, your anecdotes may sometimes involve deeply personal details, so sometimes you may later feel like you've overshared.

An example of the kind of stories or personal anecdote I enjoy sharing is _____

_____.

The people with whom I enjoy sharing personal anecdotes are _____

_____.

ENJOYING TANGENTS, LOOPS, AND FAST-PACED CONVERSATIONS

In Autistic and ADHDer social culture, having tangential, wandering conversations with frequent interruptions and loops is normal, and interrupting others so that you don't lose your train of thought is not considered rude. The form of the conversations reflects how you feel. It may be fast-paced and highly energetic if you are excited about a topic or sharing an interest, or slower and more reflective if your energy levels are lower. It can be fun to see others get fired up and passionate about things they enjoy, and it is satisfying to share your thoughts with someone who understands.

The kinds of topics that get me excited and energized are _____

_____.

The people with whom I enjoy these kinds of conversations are _____

_____.

ALLOWING SILENCE AND LOW-DEMAND SOCIALIZING

Part of Autistic and ADHDer culture includes accepting that, at times, you may be unable to speak because you are too overwhelmed and exhausted. With neurodivergent friends, you are not required to perform socially, allowing you to accommodate each other's needs by sitting silently, using sign language, or texting rather than speaking. Lowering your expectations of each other shows care and acceptance and allows each of you to self-regulate and recover in your own time.

I need silence and low-demand social contact when I feel _____

_____.

The people with whom I can socialize in low-demand ways are _____

_____.

Consider how these ways of socializing reflect your authentic needs, and identify the strategies you enjoy the most (you can check as many as you like).

Method of Social Connection	Opportunity for Joy?
Sharing Your Spins and Hyperfixations	
Diving into Detail	
Giving Penguin Pebbles	
Playing in Parallel	
Exchanging Stories and Anecdotes	
Enjoying Tangents, Loops, and Fast-Paced Conversations	
Allowing Silence and Low-Demand Socializing	

Having ways to socialize that match your needs will allow you to participate in social situations authentically, even when you have limited capacity to participate. This will make friendships more sustainable in the long term.

Find Your Neurokin

Relationships between neurodivergent and non-neurodivergent people work well when both sides are willing to listen and adapt to the other's needs. However, relationships with people who share your communication style, social preferences, identity, and values may often feel easier, and you may be more likely to feel you belong (Botha, Dibb, and Frost 2022; Cooper et al. 2021; Maroney and Horne 2022; Lilley et al. 2022; Tan 2018). In relationships with other neurodivergent people you will never feel like a "failed neurotypical." Your neurokin share your attraction to deep interests, making these friendships often easier to develop and sustain (Chan, Doran, and Galobardi 2023; Cooper et al. 2023; Crompton and Bond 2022; Crompton, Hallett, et al. 2020; Crompton, Sharp, et al. 2020; Sosnowy et al. 2019).

Finding neurokin who share your interests opens opportunities for connection by doing what you love together, and deepening your relationships with people you already know is a good place to start. List the people you know who share your interests, even if you don't know them very well yet.

_____   _____

_____   _____

_____   _____

Now, circle the names of people with whom you currently enjoy spending time, underline those you find easy to talk to, and place an * next to those you do not know well but would like to know better. You now have a shortlist of people who could become closer friends with some focused effort.

If you do not have a lot of existing social connections, you may find new friends by connecting with your interests in person or online. You could attend a community event, join a group focused on your favorite hobby, or play online with people who share your love of a game (Chan, Doran, and Galobardi 2023; Sundberg 2018).

Consider how you might like to make these connections, then fill in the following table with a range of options. You are not committed to doing anything you write here—these are just ideas for now.

My Interest	Where I Could Meet People Who Share This Interest

Consider the kind of support you would need to make these connections. For example, you might benefit from help with (check all that apply):

- ☐ Finding the information that you need

- ☐ Getting yourself organized to attend

- ☐ Making phone calls

- ☐ Finding out what to expect

- ☐ Attending the first few times

- ☐ Support while you are there

- ☐ Transport to and from the event

- ☐ Other: _____

Nurture a Small Number of Friendships

Like many ADHDers and Autistic people, you probably value fairness, loyalty, and helping others. In your friendships, you may try to be fair by treating everyone the same, but this makes it difficult to deepen any friendships beyond a superficial level. You may not realize that non-neurodivergent people have different approaches to making and managing friendships. They automatically and unconsciously prioritize some friends over others, based on how close that person is to them and a range of other intangible considerations such as the person's social status, shared interests, the usefulness of the connection, and what that person offers them in terms of support (Ball and Newman 2013).

Intuitively understanding that they can only sustain a small number of very close friends, non-neurodivergent people tend to have expanding circles of friendship, based on how close they are to each person. Their inner circle may contain just a couple of intimate friendships. From here, the circles expand to include people considered close friends, then good friends, then outward to more distant friends and people with whom they do not spend much time. You may fall into this circle if you haven't deepened your friendship with them. The outer circles include acquaintances, work colleagues, and people they've met whose names they know. The effort they put into each relationship depends on which circle the person occupies, and you will not be prioritized unless you are in one of the inner circles. This may explain why you always feel on the outer edge of your friendship group, a lonely position that can feel like a constant drip-feed of small rejections.

Even though you may want to avoid hurting or rejecting anyone, having a small group of friends that you prioritize over others is essential if you want to develop safe, supportive friendships. The key is to find the special people with whom you feel accepted and respected, then focus on deepening these connections in a targeted way. In *Unmasking Autism* (2022), Devon Price describes these special friends as his *strawberry people*.

Finding Your Strawberry People

Developing deeper connections can have a lasting positive impact on your wellbeing. The process of doing this seems quite simple on the surface, yet it will require persistence and a little courage as you put the steps into action.

Step 1: Find People Who Get You

Work out who the people are with whom you feel most at ease—those who seem to "get you" and that you enjoy being with. Look for people outside your close family, ideally neurokin who are friends or acquaintances. You may not know these people well yet, but you'd like to invest in getting to know them better. This will be quite a small number of people; ideally no more than four.

List their names here:

_____

_____

Step 2: Create a Cue for Connection

Find these people in your phone contacts or messaging apps. Attach an emoji or symbol to the end of each person's name. This symbol will show up whenever they message you. (You must open and edit their contact profiles to do this.) Use the same emoji for everyone. The emoji creates a consistent visual cue that you need to treat this friend differently from other people you know. Devon used a strawberry emoji, which is how these people became known as his strawberry people.

Draw a picture of the emoji you will use.

Step 3: Prioritize These People in Your Life

Using the emoji as a visual reminder, actively prioritize these people in your life. Reply to their texts quickly and make time to see them when possible. Tell these people you value them and enjoy spending time with them. Suggest ways that you could see each other more.

Write a brief script for how you could tell this person you enjoy their company and want to develop your friendship.

"I want to tell you that _____

_____."

Investing time and energy in seeing your strawberry people will help you deepen these connections. Describe some activities you might invite these people to do with you.

_____

_____

_____

_____

Remember that it takes time and persistent effort to establish strong friendships. With time, layers of small interactions can grow into something lasting, but without consistent effort, the connection can fade. How long it takes to develop a new friendship not only depends on how much time you spend with the person, but on how authentic you are, how much you unmask and reveal your neurodivergent differences, and whether you can find the courage to say that you value spending time with them. This is a potential shortcut to long-lasting and deep connections: unmasking and inviting the other person to do so too. In chapter 7, you will explore how to unmask and disclose your neurodivergence safely. Our hope is that you can use this as a pathway to deeper connections.

Let Go of Trying to Keep Everyone Happy

It is understandable that you would try to avoid rejection, given how painful it can be; however, doing this by trying to keep everyone happy is also problematic. When you behave as though your needs do not matter, other people will also act as if this is true. Your friendships will become uneven, with you always giving and never receiving from others. Eventually, you may start feeling selfish for expecting anything from your friendships. Yet if you always say yes, you are at risk of being manipulated into doing things that keep others happy but are hurtful to you.

I usually worry a lot about keeping everyone happy when I am out. I try to find restaurants everyone will like, and since I am good at navigating, I take responsibility for this too. I find this exhausting and stressful. However, recently I went out with some people I knew were also Autistic but whom I had only just met. That night, we told each other exactly what we wanted to eat and where we wanted to go—there was no masking, and no one took offense. We supported each other to do whatever was right for us. It was relaxing and empowering, and I made some wonderful new friends. —Jennifer

LEARNING TO SAY NO

Learning to say no to unreasonable demands is the first step to overcoming people-pleasing patterns. Saying no may seem simple on the surface, but it can be hard to do. As an act of self-compassion, you should consider saying no whenever:

- You are being asked to do something that does not feel right

- An unreasonable expectation is being placed on you

- Doing it will require more time and energy than you have available

- Doing it will harm you

- It is something someone else could easily do

- You are only doing it because you feel guilty

Saying no can be exceedingly difficult if you feel guilty, awkward, or worried about how the other person might react. You may tend to overexplain to seek forgiveness and understanding. However, saying no politely, clearly, and firmly does not need to include a long explanation. Instead, it can simply sound like:

"I'm sorry, I can't."

"I wish I could help, but I just can't on this occasion."

"I appreciate the offer, but I just can't this time."

"Thank you for thinking of me. Unfortunately, I'm not available."

"No, thank you."

Advocating for yourself by saying no gets easier with practice, but it still helps to prepare. To practice this, think about an upcoming commitment you would prefer to politely decline, then complete the following table.

Questions	Example Situation	Your Situation
Briefly describe the situation	*Whenever I visit my friend, she expects me to stay late and listen to her problems.*	
Why this is an unreasonable expectation of you	*It's too tiring, and she never asks how I am.*	
The negative impact doing this has on you	*It exhausts me for the entire next day. I feel hurt, like she doesn't care for me.*	
How you will say no in a polite, clear, and firm way	*"I'm sorry, I can't stay late tonight. I have to get up early tomorrow."*	

Questions	Example Situation	Your Situation
Uncomfortable emotions that might show up	*I feel guilty and scared that I'll lose her as a friend and be lonely.*	
How you can self-soothe while still saying no	*After I get home, I can acknowledge how hard this is for me, stim, and watch my favorite TV show.*	

Once you begin saying no more often, reflect on how it feels and what it means for you. If you find it challenging to do, note that, too; this suggests you may need more practice and support. Write down your thoughts below:

_____

_____

_____

HOLDING BOUNDARIES

Boundaries are clear statements of your valid needs, including being treated with respect and having access to time alone, quiet, privacy, and help. Boundaries are essential for your long-term wellbeing. You may not be used to holding boundaries, worry that this may cause people to be unhappy with you, or feel like this is selfish, but they are an act of self-compassion that can protect your physical and mental health. Your boundaries define:

- How you are willing to spend your limited time and energy

- What you are willing to do for someone else

- What you are willing to give (money, possessions, gifts)

- What are fair and reasonable expectations to have of you

- The behavior you will accept from others

- Who can touch your body, when this is allowed, and what they can touch

- The amount of personal space you need and when

Your boundaries can only define what is acceptable to you. They do not directly control what others do, but they can influence others' behavior by clearly defining what you will and won't accept and how you will respond if a boundary is crossed. Simply telling people your boundaries may not be enough; you need to follow through with consistent action. No one will hold your boundaries except you. Others will not change their behavior unless they realize you are serious and you hold the boundary consistently.

To implement a boundary effectively, it is helpful to prepare yourself. Consider what the person does that is upsetting, the impact that behavior has on you, and why the behavior is unacceptable, unreasonable, unwanted, and/or disrespectful. Clearly defining your boundary states your limits and the change you want to see. This also involves explaining why it is important and what the outcome will be if the boundary isn't respected.

Setting and Maintaining Boundaries

In this activity, you will develop a plan to create and hold a boundary with someone close to you. Complete the following table, then practice saying your boundary statement aloud using a calm, steady, and matter-of-fact tone before delivering it in real time. You can download a blank version of this worksheet at https://www.newharbinger.com/53073.

Questions	Example Situation	Your Situation
Person's name	Sarah	
Relationship to you	Mom	
What they do that is upsetting and unwanted	Mom always jokes about my mistakes with the rest of the family.	
Impact of their behavior on you	I feel like I am constantly failing. I feel embarrassed.	

Questions	Example Situation	Your Situation
How their behavior is unacceptable, unreasonable, unwanted, and/or disrespectful	*It feels like she expects me to be perfect, and if I'm not, I'm a joke. She should not say these things in public.*	
Your valid needs in this situation	*To be treated with respect. For my mistakes to be private.*	
Your Boundary Statement (A clear request that defines the change you'd like in their behavior and why this is important to you)	*Mom, I want you to stop making jokes about my mistakes because it makes me feel bad about myself.*	
Statement of what will happen if they cross the boundary	*If you don't stop making jokes about me, I won't share these things with you and may not come to as many family events.*	
Uncomfortable emotions that might show up	*I feel anxious that she'll get upset and shout at me.*	
Urge to avoid the uncomfortable emotions	*I want to avoid the whole conversation.*	
How you can self-soothe while still holding the boundary	*Before, I can take a few deep breaths. After, I can acknowledge how difficult this is, move my body, and listen to my favorite music.*	
Helpful support available to you	*I can talk to a close friend if I feel upset.*	

Once you've stated your boundary, briefly describe how it felt to deliver this. Note how the other person responded, and outline your next steps.

_____

_____

_____

_____

_____

_____

_____

Unfortunately, setting boundaries about what you will and won't accept is sometimes not enough to change a person's behavior. Creating a more substantial boundary may be necessary to limit how much this person hurts you. It can be painful when this happens. You may grieve the loss of friends or family members you no longer see and feel resentful that they would not change, even though they may have been toxic relationships for you.

Fortunately, you can create safe relationships with people who accept, support, trust, and respect you. Friendships with neurokin who share your interests will take less effort and be more sustainable in the long term. By becoming a better friend for yourself, you can also access an ongoing source of warmth, acceptance, and kindness as you work toward forming these safe connections. We hope you can use skills outlined in this chapter to create a close group of safe friendships with people who accept you as you are.

CHAPTER 7

Unmasking Safely and Finding Who You Are

> Refusing to perform neurotypicality is a revolutionary act of disability justice.
> It's also a radical act of self-love.
>
> —Devon Price, *Unmasking Autism: The Power*
> *of Embracing Our Hidden Neurodiversity*

Concealing your differences and performing a version of yourself that others will accept are learned survival skills in a society that does not respect or accept your differences. The more intersectional differences you have from the majority, the more you must keep yourself safe from microaggressions, bullying, stigma, ableism, and exclusion. If you've been masking since childhood, your performance may have become so nuanced, sophisticated, and automatic that you may not even be aware you are doing it.

Unmasking is the process of "allowing yourself to be a normal neurodivergent person, not an abnormal neurotypical" (Tan 2018) and, ultimately, is the only viable pathway to self-acceptance and self-compassion. Even though you will still need to mask in some situations, the way to a fulfilling life is to learn how to be you. The more you can unmask, accept your differences, and appreciate your neurodivergent identity, the greater your life satisfaction will be (Bargiela, Steward, and Mandy 2016; Botha, Dibb, and Frost 2022; Lilley et al. 2022). In this chapter, you will learn practical strategies to unmask safely. You'll explore how to find people you can trust, plan what you will say when you reveal your neurodivergence to others, and find opportunities to gently drop your mask when it is safe to do so.

Why Masking Doesn't Work

As Brené Brown has said, "Fitting in is one of the greatest barriers to belonging" (Brown 2015). In friendships where you are masking, you shoulder the burden of making the relationship work by fitting yourself into other people's expectations. Building on a foundation of pretense guarantees that your friendship will remain superficial, and you will never feel like you belong. It is impossible to accept yourself if you need to pretend to be someone else; you can easily lose sight of who you are and what you need.

No matter how often and fluently you mask, even the most elegant performance will have tiny flaws. Others can sense these quirks in your behavior, and it doesn't take much to make people pause. One recent study by Sasson et al. (2017) found that nonautistic people tend to be less willing to spend time with Autistic people based on just a few seconds of observed behavior. The nonautistic participants did not know the person they were watching was Autistic, but based on these "thin slice judgments," they were less likely to want to hang out, sit next to, and talk to them. They also found the Autistic people less likable and attractive (Sasson et al. 2017). This phenomenon makes friendships with non-neurodivergent people much more difficult to navigate. Furthermore, whenever you are under pressure, tired, drinking, or using other substances, your slight differences become more noticeable. This makes you more vulnerable to teasing or mocking, even if you have no idea what you've done wrong.

When you've been masking who you are for a long time, you can begin to worry that you will be found out (Cage and Troxell-Whitman 2019), and may invest so much energy in your social performance that you constantly feel anxious and distracted. You may also become more fatigued, have more frequent headaches, and have greater difficulty concentrating. Social situations will feel more disjointed, awkward, and exhausting—the exact outcome you'd rather avoid. No wonder masking is closely linked to social anxiety (Hull et al. 2021). In addition, if you have no choice but to mask, it can also contribute to depression, isolation, lower self-esteem, suicidal thoughts, self-harming behavior, and a feeling of loneliness even when you are with people (Bargiela, Steward, and Mandy 2016; Cage and Troxell-Whitman 2019; Cassidy et al. 2018; Cassidy et al. 2020; Evans, Krumrei-Mancuso, and Rouse 2023).

I was diagnosed Autistic at 40. Rather than feeling relief, I was angry. I did not believe the diagnosis at first. No one had ever told me I was weird or different, only that I was extremely quiet and shy. Growing up, I never tried to copy other people's behavior to fit in, but I now realize I was masking. Growing up in Asia, where being a quiet and studious child is valued, I hid my differences by withdrawing in social situations. This way, I never drew anyone's attention. It helped me get through school, but the challenges I faced in silence have become bigger mental health problems later in life. —Esther

Describe the difficulties masking has caused you, including any impact on your sense of identity, emotional distress, and mental health problems.

_____

_____

_____

_____

Once you begin to unmask, you may resent the energy it takes to keep everyone happy. Despite the impact on your mental health and wellbeing, you must weigh the burden of masking against the potential for bullying and rejection if you don't. You are stuck between two uncomfortable options: be yourself and risk others not liking you, or keep up a performance that is draining and unsatisfying for you. The only pathway you can take through these difficulties starts with learning who you will become when you unmask.

Learning Who You Are by Unmasking to Yourself

As soon as you consider unmasking, you may wonder what being yourself would look and feel like. When you've been hiding who you are for a long time, it can be challenging to know who *you* are. Simply asking yourself, "Who am I?" may not offer much clarity either (Artemisia 2018). The neuronormative way to answer this question is to describe one or more of your important social identities based on gender, race, ethnic minority, sexual orientation, nationality, religion, disability status, career, political orientation, family, or parental status (Vance 2021). Using this approach, the answer to "Who are you?" sounds brief and factual, such as "I am a Christian mom of two," or "I am a special education teacher at an Illinois state school."

That might be a suitable response for some, but for many neurodivergent people, it may not be a satisfying answer because you know that your identity is much more than your social roles. Who you are is flexible, adaptable, and constantly changing. Autistic people, and many ADHDers too, tend to understand their identity through what they love to do (interests), what is important to them (values), and their life experiences (personal stories). As a neurodivergent person, if you are asked, "Who are you?" you are likely to describe what you are passionate about or interested in, such as, "I am a music lover," "I am a research scientist," "I am a writer," "I am an animal rights activist," or "I am an educator" (Vance 2021). This flexible view of identity defines who you are as an ongoing and active process of what you love and what you do that evolves throughout your life.

Over the following pages, you will have an opportunity to reflect on your identity from four perspectives that, when put together, will help you unmask to yourself and understand who you are. You will explore:

1. What is important to you: your values

2. The personal qualities you want to express when you are with other people

3. What you enjoy doing: your interests

4. The *you* that is always present, constant and unchanging

Let's look at each of these in turn.

What's Important to You: Your Values

Values are verbs—they are something you do. Your values are not goals you can complete; rather, they are an ongoing process of considering what is important to you and making choices about how you will behave. Living a life aligned with your values brings meaning and satisfaction to your life (Hayes, Strosahl, and Wilson 2016; Twohig, Levin, and Ong 2021).

Your values guide your choices; they describe how you want to live, where you want to invest your energy, and how you will behave when you are with others. They will be reflected in the people you choose to spend time with and your contributions to others, the community, and the world. Values are not about how others treat you, so "being respected" or "being loved" are not values. Instead, values reflect what *you* do, such as "being loving" and "respecting others" (Stoddard and Afari 2014). Only you can choose your values. They describe what is important to you, not how others want you to behave or what you must do to keep people happy. You should never have to justify your values, nor should they reflect the social rules you are expected to follow (Twohig, Levin, and Ong 2021; Wilson and Dufrene 2010).

It can help you connect with your values by considering the legacy you'd like to leave behind when you reach the end of your life. To try this, complete the following sentences:

At the end of my life, I would like people to describe me as _____, _____,

_____, and _____.

As I approach the final days of my life, the things that will feel the most meaningful to me will be

_____ and _____.

The people I want to help the most in my life are _____, _____,

_____, and _____.

The "Sweet Spot" exercise is a lovely way to explore your values by reflecting on a meaningful and enriching experience in your past (Hayes, Strosahl, and Wilson 2016; Stoddard and Afari 2014). It can help you understand how your values infuse every aspect of your life.

The Sweet Spot

Think about a time when you felt fully engaged in something meaningful and joyful. In this sweet moment, you felt deeply fulfilled and satisfied. You might have been engrossed in your spin, enjoying a happy moment with your child or friend, or moving your body in a pleasant way. Whatever it is, there's a lightness in this moment, and your struggles have faded into the background. You are in the "sweet spot."

Remember one sweet spot experience you've had in as much detail as possible. If you notice that you are searching your mind for the "best" example for this exercise, try to let go of this struggle and instead focus on describing one pleasant experience you remember well. Describe:

Where you were: _____

_____

What you were doing: _____

_____

Who you were with: _____

_____

How you felt: _____

_____

Describe the emotions and physical sensations you notice inside your body while you remember your sweet spot. You may like to refer to the list of emotions in chapter 6 as a guide.

Emotion: _____ Physical sensation: _____

Emotion: _____ Physical sensation: _____

Emotion: _____ Physical sensation: _____

Pay attention to any self-critical thoughts during this exercise, such as, "I'm not doing this properly" or "I don't have a sweet enough memory." Write these down too, then let them go for now.

_____

_____

_____

_____

The experiences in your life that give you the most joy, satisfaction, and contentment are those closely aligned with your values. The domains in which people tend to hold important values are listed below. Place checkmarks indicating which valued domains were reflected in your sweet spot, adding others in the space provided:

☐ Connecting with others (family, friendships, intimate relationships)

☐ Parenting

☐ Time alone

☐ Helping others and advocacy

☐ Work and achievement

☐ Learning

☐ Creativity

☐ Physical and mental wellbeing

☐ Community connections

☐ Home environment

☐ Spiritual beliefs and faith

☐ Personal growth

☐ Other: _____

Inside your story are clues about what is important to you. To discover this, complete one or more of the following sentences:

What was special in that moment of my life was _____

_____.

What is deeply important to me is _____

_____.

Something worth more than anything to me is _____

_____ .

I could never give up _____

_____ .

The sweet spot exercise can shine a light on the joys in your life and what is deeply important to you. You can repeat this exercise with any beautiful moment in your life. Each will contain clues about what you yearn for and could never give up, and can therefore give you helpful guidance on what to prioritize in your life.

If you have always needed to mask who you are, you may have had to follow other people's values and priorities rather than your own. It can feel extremely uncomfortable if other people want you to behave in ways that don't sit right with you. Many Autistic people and ADHDers have deeply held values related to social justice, fairness, loving connections, and helping others, both human and animal. That means you place greater importance on living according to your values rather than following social norms and hierarchies. You may be willing to speak up about issues related to these values, even if it makes you unpopular or causes conflict. Many whistleblowers are Autistic truth-tellers who simply could not do something they did not believe was right (Vance 2021).

Place an X on the line to reflect the extent to which you live according to other people's values or your own.

I make choices based on what other people believe is important.   I make choices based on what is important to me.

Standing up for what is important can fill you with pride and deep satisfaction. It can also be painful if others are upset with you, resulting in complicated feelings of shame, embarrassment, and regret. Ultimately, the choice is to live according to your values and risk making others upset, or be unhappy because you are living in a way that feels inauthentic. This can be a difficult and sometimes painful choice to make.

Express Who You Are with Others

As Margery Williams so beautifully explored in her children's book *The Velveteen Rabbit*, we become "real" (our authentic selves) through our relationships with other people and understand ourselves through how these people see us (Williams 2004). Moment by moment, the personal qualities you express will unfold differently depending on who you are with and what you are doing. You get to choose the person you want to be with others and align your actions with your deeply held values.

Listed below are personal qualities that many people value. Circle the personal qualities that resonate for you. Then, place an * next to up to eight qualities that feel essential to who you are.

Personal Qualities Many People Value

Accepting	Energetic	Joyful	Respectful
Adventurous	Enthusiastic	Kind	Responsible
Appreciative	Equitable	Knowledgeable	Risk-taking
Approachable	Fair	Loving	Safe
Assertive	Faithful	Loyal	Self-sufficient
Attentive	Fearless	Nonjudgmental	Serene
Authentic	Forgiving	Nurturing	Soothing
Aware	Focused	Open	Spiritual
Bold	Free	Optimistic	Spontaneous
Calm	Friendly	Organized	Stable
Caring	Fun	Passionate	Strong
Collaborative	Funny	Patient	Structured
Compassionate	Generous	Peaceful	Successful
Competent	Gentle	Persistent	Supportive
Connected	Giving	Playful	Thorough
Consistent	Grateful	Positive	Thoughtful
Courageous	Helpful	Powerful	Tolerant
Creative	Honest	Practical	Trusting
Curious	Honorable	Present	Understanding
Decisive	Imaginative	Proactive	Warm
Determined	Independent	Productive	Welcoming
Disciplined	Inspirational	Reliable	Wise
Encouraging	Intuitive	Respectable	Witty

Living Your Values

In this activity, you will define how you approach aspects of your life by considering the personal qualities you would like to express in specific situations. Each sentence below relates to a different value domain. Complete each sentence using the qualities listed above as a guide. Some qualities may apply to multiple domains, and some domains may not apply to you; if so, leave it and move on to the next.

Connecting with Others

When I am with my family, the personal qualities I like to express are _____,

_____, and _____.

I like my friends to see me as someone _____, _____,

and _____.

With my intimate partner(s), it's important to me to be _____, _____,

and _____.

I aim to be _____, _____, and _____ in conflict situations or with difficult people.

It's important to me to treat all people and animals with _____, _____,

and _____.

Parenting

It's important to me to be a parent who is _____, _____,

and _____.

I would like my children to see me as someone who is _____, _____,

and _____.

Time Alone

When I'm alone, the personal qualities I most enjoy expressing are _____,

_____, and _____.

Spending regular time alone helps me be someone who is _____,

_____, and _____.

Helping Others and Advocacy

When advocating for others, I aim to be _____, _____, and

_____.

I aim to be _____, _____, and _____ when
I'm looking after people or animals.

Work and Achievement

When I'm at work I like to be _____, _____, and

_____.

I approach my goals with _____, _____, and

_____.

Learning

I aim to approach learning opportunities with _____, _____,

and _____.

Creativity

Expressing myself creatively involves me being _____, _____,

and _____.

Physical and Mental Wellbeing

I aim to be _____, _____, and _____ when
I'm looking after my physical and mental health.

Community Connections

The personal qualities I like to express when I'm participating in community events are

_____, _____, and _____.

I like to be someone who is _____, _____, and

_____ when contributing to my community.

Home Environment

At home, I like to be _____, _____, and

_____.

When I have things organized at home, it allows me to be _____,

_____, and _____.

Spiritual Beliefs and Faith

As I practice my spiritual beliefs or faith, it's important to me to be _____,

_____, and _____.

Personal Growth

As I continue to grow as a person, I would like to be someone who is _____,

_____, and _____.

To finish this exercise, review your answers and highlight any themes you find in your chosen qualities. For example, you may notice a theme of compassion in personal qualities, such as being kind, warm, patient, and accepting. A theme related to achievement might appear as terms like competent, determined, passionate, and organized. Or a playfulness theme might show up as words like fun, witty, imaginative, and spontaneous.

Summarize up to five values themes below. These clusters reflect how you express your values in daily life.

_____

_____

_____

_____

_____

Your values remain consistent, even when your behavior must change to fit the situation. Use the values themes you've identified above to guide you in unmasking and being authentic with others.

You Are What You Do

Whether you are fascinated with a rare insect, experience deep pleasure exploring complex transport systems, can't get enough of true crime stories, or know everything there is to know about your favorite pop band, your spins and hyperfixations are a constant source of joy. As Autistic advocate and actor Chloe Hayden writes in her book *Different, Not Less: A Neurodivergent's Guide to Embracing Your True Self and Finding Your Happily Ever After*, your interests—what she calls "eye sparkles"—enrich and give meaning to your life and make you feel energized, powerful, and happy (Hayden 2022). It's time to start appreciating your interests as things that reflect who you are as a person, too.

Celebrating Your "Eye Sparkles"

In this activity, you will explore your interests and link them to your unmasked identity. Consider the spins and hyperfixations that give you immense joy, then complete the following sentences.

A much-loved interest I've had since childhood is _____

_____.

A collection (physical or online) that is meaningful for me is _____

_____.

An interest that has influenced my career path is _____

_____.

An interest that has helped me build friendships is _____

_____.

An interest that has helped me learn about myself is _____

_____.

Consider your experience of spending time in your interests and complete the following sentences:

When I am deeply engrossed in my interests, the personal qualities I am expressing are

_____, _____, and _____.

When I can spend regular time focused on my interests, I am _____,

_____, and _____.

Whether through your work, writing, singing, drawing, painting, crafts, dancing, sport, teaching, modeling, gaming, or use of technology, find ways to deepen your connection with these sources of joy. Outline any ideas you have for new ways to connect with your interests.

_____

_____

_____

_____

It's time to do more of what energizes and inspires you (Artemisia 2018). Your interests do not need to make you money or be a successful "side hustle" to be valid and worthy of your time. Celebrating and sharing your interests will connect you to a deep sense of satisfaction and is a pathway to greater wellbeing and self-acceptance (Price 2022).

Meeting the You at the Heart of It All

Philosophers have argued for centuries about the nature of self-awareness and consciousness, but we will sidestep this debate and simply note that a part of you is always watching your experiences. This is your *observing self*. Your life experiences and what you do are constantly changing, but this unwavering presence watches your ever-changing experience. As such, your observing self sits at the heart of who you are.

To connect with this consistent, ever-present part of yourself, look back to the sweet spot you wrote about earlier. Read the description of your sweet spot aloud (this is important) as if you are telling the story to a friend. As you read, notice the part of you that is listening to your voice as you speak. Now, read your self-critical thoughts aloud and notice that once again, a part of you is listening. This part of you is noticing how you feel and listening to your thoughts, too.

As you already noticed in the chapter 4 exercise *Weather in the Sky*, part of you is always present and unchanging. Your observing self is like the sky, with the continuous stream of actions, feelings, opinions, judgments, and evaluations (in other words, everything you do) as the weather. The sky never changes; it is always there, no matter whether a storm is raging or peaceful clouds drift by. When you can watch your emotions and thoughts from a distance, as something that's passing by like the weather, they have less impact on you. You do not have to believe your thoughts or allow them to control your response.

Unfortunately, it can be easy to lose sight of your values and be disappointed in your behavior. In those moments, when you are more rude, impatient, irritable, or judgmental than you would like, you are not being the version of yourself you want to be. Living your values is an ongoing, active, and imperfect process that can be difficult to navigate. Whenever this happens, your task is to gently, kindly get yourself back on track and try again.

Navigating Unmasking Safely

Unfortunately, we still live in a society where there is stigma attached to Autism and ADHD, and your experience of unmasking will depend on your relative level of privilege or disadvantage. If you have financial security, a supportive family, and secure work, you may be able to unmask in most or all areas of your life. If, however, you belong to other minorities such as being BIPoC or LGBTQIA+, have additional disabilities, or do not have stable housing or employment, this process will be more difficult.

The key is to unmask safely, and there are four parts to this:

1. Finding people with whom you are safe to unmask

2. Planning how you will discuss your neurodivergent identity

3. Choosing your approach to neuronormative social rules

4. Gently putting down your mask to make more authentic choices

However fast or slow this process is for you, start by unmasking only with safe people that you feel confident will understand and appreciate you as you are.

Unmask with Safe People

Everyone navigates unmasking differently. When you first realize you are neurodivergent, you may want to tell everyone, share it with a few close people, or hide it altogether. Whenever you decide to share your neurodivergence with others, it's worth considering who you will tell and how safe this will be. It can be challenging to work out who is a safe person. Look for people who:

- Treat others with kindness and respect no matter their background or disability

- Speak respectfully about others when they are not there

- Demonstrate openness and curiosity about individual differences

- Are willing to adapt their behavior to meet others' needs and preferences

- Demonstrate that they value social justice and equality in their daily actions

Consider who meets these criteria in your life and complete the following sentence:

The people with whom I feel safe to unmask are _____, _____,

and _____.

Not everyone is going to be accepting. Some people may need time to understand what your neurodivergence means. Others may be open-minded but not know how to respond in an affirming way, which can lead to awkward, disappointing, and hurtful conversations (Campbell 2018). Consider who these people may be and complete the following sentence:

The people with whom it is safest to stay masked are _____, _____,

and _____.

Place an X on the line to reflect the reactions you've had from others when you've disclosed your neurodivergence.

I have had mostly invalidating and
disappointing reactions.

I have had mostly validating and
affirming reactions.

Unfortunately, sharing your neurodivergence can sometimes lead to a permanent rift in a relationship if the person completely rejects your identity. In situations where you must manage how people perceive you, such as at work, you must be particularly thoughtful about whether you share your neurodivergence and how you do it. Many employers do not know how to accommodate the needs of neurodivergent employees, and this can have unwanted implications for you (Kidwell, Clancy, and Fisher 2023).

Therefore, before you begin to unmask, it's essential to consider the risks. Complete the following table by listing the people with whom you'd like to share your neurodivergent identity. Describe the potential benefits and risks of sharing your identity for each person.

Person	Possible Benefits of Unmasking	Possible Risks of Unmasking

Person	Possible Benefits of Unmasking	Possible Risks of Unmasking

Disclosing your neurodivergence is a form of "coming out," and it's not for everyone (Campbell 2018). Since you can never be entirely sure how people will respond, it is helpful to be ready for the conversation.

Consider Your Approach to Disclosure

The best possible outcome for your conversation is the other person clearly understanding and accepting what your neurodivergence means to you. However, it is likely that you will have several negative experiences when revealing your neurodivergent identity. These can shake your confidence and leave you feeling vulnerable and uncertain. Whether intentional or not, stigma communicated by others can also trigger feelings of shame within you. If you fully accept your neurodivergent spiky profile, it will make these conversations easier. You will be able to express yourself more confidently and not take on board other people's negative views. You can also increase the chances of the conversation being successful by:

- Using concise and affirming language

- Clearly describing what being neurodivergent means to you

- Modeling self-acceptance in how you describe yourself

- Being prepared to answer questions and concerns

- Having factual and straightforward responses ready for invalidating statements

As with anything, it helps to prepare. Complete the following plan to prepare yourself for unmasking conversations that are confident and model self-acceptance.

Describing Your Neurodivergent Identity or Diagnosis	
Your identity-first description ("I am…")	
Your preferred affirming language choices	
Explaining What Your Neurodivergence Means to You	
What being neurodivergent means for you day-to-day	
Strengths that form part of your spiky profile	
Challenges your neurodivergence can cause	
Troubleshooting	
What their concerns or fears might be	
Question(s) they may ask	
Your response	

Many of the more invalidating responses made by parents and loved ones come from a concern about what this diagnosis might mean for you in the future, or fear about what this might mean for them. Even if they react negatively initially, it may not be how they feel forever. People need time to adapt, and it will help if you can demonstrate how this identity is a positive thing for you.

If the person you disclose to responds in a disappointing or invalidating way, it will be easier to manage if you have a thoughtful and assertive response ready. Here are some ways you can respond to invalidating statements in a straightforward and confident manner.

Invalidating Statements	Confident, Positive, and Straightforward Responses
"Everyone is a little bit on the spectrum."	"Not really. Some people have genetic differences that result in their bodies and brains processing information differently. That applies to me too."
"It's just a fad. Everyone seems to have ADHD/Autism now."	"Yes, many people are seeing this in themselves for the first time. It's part of a big movement to destigmatize neurodivergence in our community by understanding how different it can look in people."
"You can't have Autism because you can hold eye contact/are so good to talk to."	"Thank you, yes, I am. I am Autistic, but I've put a lot of effort into fitting in. It's called masking, and while I might do it well, it's also exhausting."
"You can't have ADHD because you finished school/have a job/degree..."	"Yes, I'm proud of what I've achieved. I've put a lot of effort into this, and being an ADHDer has made this incredibly challenging."
"Your symptoms just come from trauma."	"Yes, I have experienced trauma, but I'm also Autistic/an ADHDer. This has always been part of me and is largely genetic."
"You can't have ASD because you are not like my cousin with Autism."	"Every Autistic person is different, and many have additional challenges. One of the features of my Autistic profile is how much I mask my difficulties."
"You don't have ADHD; you just take on too many things."	"Yes, I am a busy person. Part of ADHD is always needing new challenges, and unfortunately, it can make me burn out."
"It's just an excuse."	"I don't agree. Identifying as neurodivergent is not making an excuse; it's about acknowledging why things are more difficult for me and asking for the help I need to succeed."

If you do not feel safe to unmask with everyone right now, that is okay. Do not criticize yourself for this; your highest priority needs to be keeping yourself safe. You can return to these pages whenever you are ready to start these conversations.

Choose Your Approach to Social Rules

Everyone is assumed to know the many unspoken rules and expectations in our society. This "hidden curriculum" is never explicitly taught, yet others will judge you on how well you follow these rules (Myles,

Trautman, and Schelvan 2013). You can often learn these rules by watching what other people do; however, sometimes you won't know what is expected until you unintentionally break the hidden rules and others are surprised, confused, or upset with you.

Trying to follow neuronormative social rules and meet other people's expectations can be exhausting and perplexing, particularly when you don't understand what people want and those rules do not make much sense to you. However, you can choose the extent to which you follow these rules or make your own choices about what is the right thing to do. Choosing to be different in a way that feels authentic to you is a form of unmasking.

Listed below are some common yet usually unspoken neuronormative social rules. For each rule, indicate whether or not you choose to follow this rule.

Common Neuronormative Social Rules	Will You Follow This?
If someone asks, "How are you?" you must answer, "Fine, thanks," no matter how you feel.	
It is acceptable to lie to avoid hurting someone's feelings, even if you lie to them directly.	
If your viewpoint or situation changes, you do not have to do something you've committed to.	
If someone has a problem with their appearance, such as food stuck between their teeth or their clothing label is showing, you should ignore it and not tell them.	
Don't correct people when they make mistakes, even if it would help them.	
Accept someone's strong beliefs even if they don't have logical reasons for them.	
Do not ask people why they are doing something—this is considered rude and aggressive.	
You must hold just the right amount of eye contact when you are speaking to someone—but not so much that it's weird.	
If you do not get to make your point during a conversation, just forget about it because you won't get to say it at all.	
Always ask follow-up questions about a person's story and do not share a similar thing that happened to you.	
Always follow unspoken rules, unless there's a reason you can't follow them; then you don't have to.	

Now that you've read some of the hidden curriculum, reflect on what your responses reveal about how much you currently follow these hidden social rules and how you'd like to approach this in the future.

_____

_____

_____

_____

Sadly, if you spend a great deal of time following rules that don't make sense or trying to meet social expectations that aren't clearly stated, you may often feel like you are failing. Even if you try to read other people's social signals and adapt to fit the situation, following neuronormative rules can be tricky if they do not make logical sense. It can also be highly frustrating when people are inconsistent, do not follow through on their commitments, or behave unfairly. Even if you can't change the rules, you can choose how *you* will manage social situations in a way that feels logical, authentic, and aligned with what is important to you.

Gently Put Down Your Mask

You've probably been hiding parts of your identity and performing a persona for a long time. To ensure that others accept you, you may have developed many ways to manage other people's perceptions. Expressing who you are will require you to unwind these subtle habits. Make changes slowly to give yourself a chance to get used to being more authentically you. The people closest to you will also need time to adjust. As your new self unfolds, your approach to life will become more consistent with who you are.

As I got older, I started to become more interested in people, and after starting my special interest in psychology I learned how to mask and appear "normal." The experience of masking is exhausting: I must monitor my eye contact, smile more, animate my face more, have a more high-pitched voice, laugh now, ask the right question, keep the conversation going... Afterward, I collapse and need a lot of time to recover. Sometimes it helps to dive into a novel and at other times I just need quiet and rest. As I have gotten older it feels strange to unmask, to go back to my childhood, but it is freeing. —Monique

What you do when you are most comfortable may reflect your unmasked self, and as you unmask you may choose to start doing these things more. Think about what you do when you are most relaxed, such as when you are on your own, spending time with a close friend, or relaxing with your pet. Place a checkmark next to any items that reflect the small daily choices you make.

When alone and most comfortable, do you:

☐ Make noises

☐ Stim unashamedly

☐ Move about a lot

☐ Sit with your legs up

☐ Lie in unusual positions

☐ Wear more or less colorful clothing

☐ Wear more comfortable clothing

☐ Offer limited or no eye contact

☐ Speak more, less, or not at all

☐ Wear no underwear, shoes, or make-up

☐ Become utterly engrossed in your spins

☐ Spend time not interacting with anyone

☐ Speak completely honestly

☐ State exactly what you need

☐ Other: _____

☐ Other: _____

Letting go of your social performance is a gentle process of changing small behaviors and unwinding unhelpful habits. Consider any alternative behaviors that feel more consistent with your identity. Complete the table below by describing the masking behaviors you want to change. We've included some examples to get you started. Remember that you do not need to make all these changes—just start with one or two.

Masking Behavior	Unmasked Example	Your Authentic, Unmasked Choice
Suppressing		
Never sharing your opinions or asking for what you need	*Ask your friends for a small accommodation, such as moving to a quieter location when you are out.*	
Suppressing your urges, gestures, mannerisms, and stims	*Use your favorite fidget toy in front of friends.*	
Hiding your enthusiasm for your interests	*Allow yourself to get excited when sharing your spin, perhaps asking a friend, "Can I tell you a few of my favorite facts about that?"*	

Masking Behavior	Unmasked Example	Your Authentic, Unmasked Choice
Suppressing your sense of humor and urge to laugh	*Let out a chuckle when you find something funny.*	
Camouflaging		
Copying other people's gestures and mannerisms	*Let yourself stim in front of your friends.*	
Portraying a "more likable" persona	*Stop cracking jokes and forcing yourself to smile. Let your face soften.*	
Repeating famous quotes or in-jokes	*Share a few of your own thoughts too.*	
Laughing when you don't find something funny	*Smile but not laugh—unless it's a joke at your expense, then you don't have to smile.*	
Compensating		
Holding eye contact that feels uncomfortable or distracting	*Return eye contact only when it feels comfortable to you.*	
Restricting how often and how much you speak	*Let yourself talk passionately about your topic for a bit longer than usual.*	
Changing your facial expressions, body language, or tone of voice to make your emotions more visible	*Allow your face to relax into a more natural, neutral expression.*	
Asking questions to avoid talking about yourself	*Share one or two details about something you personally enjoy.*	

Treating this like an experiment can be helpful. As you try out these alternative behaviors, notice how you feel and note anything that feels good. Aim to do more of what feels aligned with your values, even if it feels a little awkward or unfamiliar at first.

Learning to Be You

All this time, you've been responding to subtle and not-so-subtle messages about what is and what isn't acceptable behavior. Realizing that you have behaved inconsistently with who you are can be painful. Suddenly you notice that you have been changing who you are, suppressing your needs, and bending yourself into a shape that fits what others expect. You also realize how exhausting and anxiety-provoking this is for you and how quickly masking drains your social battery.

Learning how to express your authentic needs and preferences starts with gradually unmasking to yourself. This process is full of uncertainty. You may not know how to be *you*, nor whether others will accept you if you change. The outcomes are uncertain, too. When you unmask, you may lose people from your life who can only accept your mask, not who you are. These people may prefer the version of you that prioritizes their needs over your own. They are not the right friends for you, but losing them still hurts, and replacing them will take time and effort. Therefore, it is crucial to approach unmasking slowly and gently. Give yourself time to adjust. Remember to be gentle with yourself if you make mistakes or do something others think is "weird." Perhaps this is the kind of weird you wish to be.

CHAPTER 8

Creating a World That Works Best for You

When you see someone putting on his Big Boots, you
can be pretty sure that an Adventure is going to happen.

—A. A. Milne, *Winnie-the-Pooh*

Self-advocacy is the ability to ask for what you need and express yourself without fear of judgment and discrimination. Unfortunately, our society currently does not make it easy to be yourself. Unmasking is a form of self-advocacy that makes you more vulnerable to criticism from others, and defending yourself can require a lot of emotional labor. You have already explored many skills needed to advocate for yourself in this book, such as how to use affirming language, reject unattainable neuronormative expectations, set boundaries with difficult people, and say no to unreasonable demands. Learning to soothe and regulate your emotions and cope with rejection is particularly useful when advocating for yourself, helping you stay calm while expressing your needs, hold your ground while facing potential rejection, and look after yourself if your change requests are denied.

> For me, self-advocacy is asking for the light to be turned down, walking into a venue with my
> sunglasses and earplugs on, using my fidget toys to help me concentrate, standing up so I can move
> around, and dressing in my favorite color (pink). I'll also ask to go to lunch at a quiet place or one that
> I know, and leave a social event before I am overstimulated. At home, I tell my partner when I cannot
> do things such as cook dinner or go out. This is how I show people that on the inside I do struggle and
> that I cannot do it all. —Monique

Armed with an understanding of your rights, in this chapter you'll put what you've already learned together with some final skills needed to help you create a life you love. You'll learn how to express what you need calmly and assertively, what to say when you meet resistance, and identify when to cut your losses and walk away. You'll set some practical and achievable goals to create positive changes in your life. But before you can advocate for yourself, you'll need to overcome your hesitancy to ask for help.

Why It's So Difficult to Ask for What You Need

Advocating for yourself is challenging. Whenever you clearly state your needs or ask for changes, you are at risk of being dismissed or rejected. If you've concealed your difficulties so well that others aren't aware of them, your requests may initially be met with disbelief and confusion. Other hurtful responses include complete denial, stonewalling, passive resistance, and trying to instill fear, obligation, and guilt in you (Cook and Purkis 2022; Forward and Frazier 2019). You will likely experience these as painful rejections and may have a powerful urge to give up or hide.

Consider how you feel when people disregard or dismiss your requests for support and circle any of the listed emotions that resonate with you, adding any others in the spaces provided.

Angry	Fearful	Overlooked
Anxious	Frustrated	Ridiculed
Ashamed	Helpless	Uncomfortable
Betrayed	Hopeless	Unimportant
Confused	Hurt	Unsafe
Devastated	Ignored	_____
Disregarded	Indifferent	_____
Embarrassed	Invalidated	_____

It's understandable that you might hold back from advocating for yourself when the reactions you get from others can be so hurtful. Being acknowledged and supported by others is an integral part of living a more comfortable and satisfying life, but acceptance isn't always easy to find. However, if your hesitation prevents you from asking for help, it will also prevent you from receiving it.

Overcoming the Barriers to Asking for Help

Asking for help is an act of self-compassion, and in this activity, you will uncover why it can be so difficult to do. Place a checkmark next to any of the following statements that reflect your thoughts, beliefs, and fears about advocating for yourself.

Genuine fears, concerns, and skill gaps:

☐ I am concerned that if people say no, I will be stuck with no other options.

☐ It will hurt too much if people say no.

☐ I've been hiding my difficulties for so long that I don't know what help I need.

☐ Asking for help would make me too soft, weak, or vulnerable.

☐ I don't know how to ask for help.

☐ Other: _____

Learned unhelpful beliefs:

☐ In the past my requests have been ignored or rejected, so I expect it will happen again.

☐ People have judged me when I've asked for help before.

☐ I am "not disabled enough" to need help.

☐ Asking for help is unfair when others need help but are not given it.

☐ People will bully or judge me if I get "special treatment."

☐ Other: _____

Self-judgments linked to emotional pain, shame, and guilt:

☐ Asking for accommodations would make me selfish and self-centered.

☐ I feel embarrassed asking for help; it's demeaning.

☐ I don't deserve help because it's my fault I'm finding this hard.

☐ I should be able to sort out my own problems.

☐ I just need to try harder.

☐ Other: _____

Tally the checkmarks for each category of roadblock and write down the scores below. Notice whether one area scores higher than the others or if barriers exist in all categories.

Barriers	Score
Genuine fears, concerns, and skill gaps:	
Beliefs based on your past learning:	
Self-judgments linked to emotional pain, shame, and guilt:	

Consider how you might have developed this way of thinking. Briefly describe how key people in your life have or have not advocated for their needs and what their behavior may have taught you.

_____

_____

_____

Acknowledging Your Genuine Fears, Concerns, and Skill Gaps

Your score: _____

Anytime you try something new, you can feel uncertain and awkward, so naturally, you may feel anxious about advocating for yourself. It can feel particularly uncomfortable asking for help because it immediately creates the potential for rejection. Fortunately, you've begun to learn many helpful self-advocacy skills, the most important of which is the ability to regulate your emotions. Staying calm when asking for what you need and regulating your big emotions if your request is denied will be helpful. However, self-advocacy can still be painful. You'll need to decide whether you can face this pain in the short term in the service of a bigger goal: creating a life that is satisfying, meaningful, and aligned with your values.

Describe any other strategies or skills you can use to help you manage your fears and concerns about self-advocacy.

_____

_____

Overcoming Self-Limiting Learned Unhelpful Beliefs

Your score: _____

Denying yourself help and giving yourself "tough love'" does not make things fairer for others. The only outcome is losing an opportunity to improve things for you. The reality is that you have both spiky strengths and challenges, and you have the right to accommodations that will make things more accessible and comfortable for you. You are worthy of receiving care and support, including from yourself. When you speak up and ask for support, you also encourage others to do the same. Self-advocacy can make some people uncomfortable, particularly those who benefit from things staying the same. You will need to decide whether the risk is worth it. Choose your battles and say no when you need to.

Put aside other people's needs for a moment and describe one situation where having accommodations would make things fairer and more achievable for you.

_____

_____

_____

Letting Go of Self-Judgments Linked to Emotional Pain, Shame, and Guilt

Your score: _____

"I should be able to do this" is a pervasive story among neurodivergent people, but it's time to let go of this limiting belief. Creating a world that recognizes diversity means accepting that you also face some challenges. If you choose to wear headphones and sunglasses in the supermarket, prefer to meet with friends alone rather than in large groups, or decide to leave a party early, it should not be a problem for anyone else. When the majority prioritizes their own needs over the needs of those who have a greater need for support, it is called ableism. Letting go of self-judgment and acknowledging your needs is the first step in standing up against the powerful ableism you may have internalized.

List at least three positive personal qualities you can use when advocating for yourself.

_____

_____

_____

It's time to finally stop the self-defeating pattern of trying to do everything yourself and never asking for help. Using the skills you've developed in this book, you can begin to set some goals and stretch yourself to communicate what you need clearly and assertively.

Influencing Others Through Assertive Communication

Assertive communication is the ability to speak in a way that considers and respects the rights and opinions of others while also standing up for your rights, needs, and personal boundaries (Pipaş and Jaradat 2010). Developing assertive communication skills allows you to express your thoughts and feelings, stop being manipulated or exploited, and make decisions on issues that affect your life while minimizing the risk of conflict, aggression, and jeopardizing your relationships (Lonczak 2020). Being authentic in clearly stating your needs can help others understand you better and potentially deepen your relationships.

Know Your Rights

Like everyone else, you have value and are worthy of respect and dignity. You should be able to live a life free from fear and discrimination. To speak assertively about what you need, it is helpful to understand the principles of human rights. These fundamental principles are enshrined in the _Universal Declaration of Human Rights_ (United Nations 1948) and include the right to life, the right to a fair trial, freedom from torture and other cruel and inhuman treatment, freedom of speech, freedom of religion, and the right to health, education, and an adequate standard of living.

The United Nations' _Convention on the Rights of Persons with Disabilities_ (2006) seeks to further protect and enhance the rights and opportunities of the estimated 650 million disabled people worldwide. The rights that you have under this convention include equal rights to education and employment, access to your cultural life, the right to own and inherit property, not to be discriminated against in marriage, and not to be unwilling subjects in medical experiments.

In the United States, all individuals, whether disabled or not, have certain rights in the workplace. These include the right to:

- Not be harassed or discriminated against because of race, color, religion, sex (including pregnancy, sexual orientation, or gender identity), national origin, disability, age (40 or older), or genetic information (including family medical history)

- Be paid fairly for your work and receive equal pay for equal work

- Return to the same position after maternity leave

- Receive *reasonable accommodations* needed due to a medical condition, disability, or religious beliefs (specific legal rights vary by state)

- Have any medical information or genetic information be kept confidential

- Report discrimination, participate in a discrimination investigation or lawsuit, or oppose discrimination without being retaliated against (punished) for doing so

The 1990 *Americans with Disabilities ACT* (ADA) made it unlawful to discriminate against someone with a disability, protecting your equal rights in education, hiring decisions, and while at work. If you have experienced discrimination due to your disability, you can file a complaint with the U.S. Equal Employment Opportunity Commission. For further information, see https://www.usa.gov/disability-rights.

Consider an area where you need to advocate for yourself. Do some research into your rights and summarize your findings here.

_____

_____

_____

_____

Find Practical Ways to Make Your Life Easier

You can make your life better in many ways, and you've explored quite a few ideas in this book so far. You may like to start by asking others for small accommodations. For example, if your friends want to go out to dinner and you find noisy environments draining, ask them to look for a quieter restaurant or go somewhere you can sit outside. If your boss wants to meet in a crowded cafe, ask to meet in a quiet office instead.

When it comes to work, I've had a pretty good run—though I do feel my years of tenure helped. I know that my rights to reasonable adjustments are protected under the law. So, I did some research and went to my manager to ask for some accommodations. The biggest change was having some flexibility in deadlines. I explained how these would support my overall wellbeing, and we agreed that I would let them know if I was running late. I've also been open about when my medication wears off, so, when possible, I'm not in important meetings when my brain isn't working at its best. The key has been self-acceptance. I had been feeling anxious going to work every day, even though I love what I do. Once I realized that I had been viewing myself as flawed, I came to accept that, although I am disabled, there's nothing wrong with me.
—Beck

Below are examples of reasonable accommodations you can request when studying or at work. Some will be easier to access than others. You may not know precisely what will help at first, so be ready to try various strategies and tell your manager or school that your needs might change.

REASONABLE ACCOMMODATIONS FOR STUDENTS

If you are currently a student, then it's essential to let your institution know and have an access or disability plan put in place. This will make it easier for you to get support. Place a checkmark next to any of the reasonable accommodations listed that would be helpful for you.

- ☐ Clearly articulated course expectations and the ability to have this clarified as needed

- ☐ Extra time to complete assignments if needed

- ☐ Extra time in exams, or, more helpfully, the ability to have breaks with the total elapsed time you spend working on the exam tracked

- ☐ Learning materials in alternative formats, such as having videos with subtitles, written transcripts of lectures, or audio recordings that you can listen to and rewind if needed

- ☐ Having exams in small, quiet rooms

- ☐ Having access to peer note-takers in lectures or exams

- ☐ Alternative options for class presentations, such as prerecording your presentation and giving it to the lecturer to watch privately

- ☐ Being able to choose a tutor that you feel comfortable with and change if needed

☐ The ability to fidget, move your body, stim, wear headphones, or take breaks whenever you need

☐ The ability to choose whom you work with in group assignments or complete the work on your own

REASONABLE ACCOMMODATIONS AT WORK

If you work in an environment that often overwhelms you, there may be ways to change it. Place a checkmark next to any of the reasonable accommodations listed below that would be helpful for you.

☐ Working in quiet, private spaces rather than in open-plan workspaces

☐ Working from home

☐ Having bright lights dimmed or natural rather than fluorescent lights. You can also get covers for overhead lights in open-plan offices for the light above your desk.

☐ Being given work that uses your strengths such as detail focus, systems thinking, or problem-solving

☐ Being given support in areas of greater difficulty, such as time management or administration

☐ Adjusting the brightness of your screen

☐ Working uninterrupted and wearing noise-cancelling headphones

☐ Wearing comfortable clothing

☐ Playing music, videos, or podcasts through headphones

☐ Stimming as much as you need, such as knitting, crocheting, or playing with fidget toys

☐ Adjusting your work hours, such as starting and finishing early or late

☐ Having meetings that are less frequent or shorter, with a clearly defined duration and agenda, and are held in quiet rooms

☐ Leaving your camera off in online meetings so you can move around freely

☐ Being allowed "sensory breaks" where you can go outside, be in a quiet dark room, take a walk, or listen to music

☐ Eating lunch outside away from a noisy and busy lunchroom

List three important and reasonable accommodations you'd like to request in your work, study, home life, or when socializing with friends and family.

1. _____

2. _____

3. _____

Now that you have some ideas about what you'd like to change, let's focus on how you could ask for these changes assertively and effectively.

Communicate with Clarity and Respect

By expressing concern about a specific issue, action, or behavior, you communicate a need and ask for something to change. The aim of assertive communication is to share your perspective and influence people's choices and actions without threatening, withholding, or triggering conflict. The key is being clear, concise, and respectful. Ask for what you want rather than describing what you don't want. You may also like to offer a constructive resolution to the problem; others will see you as proactive and view your request more favorably if you already have a possible solution.

QUALITIES OF ASSERTIVE COMMUNICATION

Quality	Don't Say	Do Say
Clearly and politely states your need	"It would be great if I didn't have to do this all myself."	"Could you please help me with this?"
Describes the outcome you want	"Stop making a mess in the kitchen."	"Could you wipe down the counter when you are finished?"
Respectful, not shaming	"You will never get that right."	"Can we try doing that a different way?"
Direct and nonthreatening	"You are going to get in trouble if you keep doing that!"	"Please stop doing that now."
Avoids blame, shares responsibility	"This is your fault."	"Let's find a way to fix this."
Noncritical of yourself	"I'm just hopeless at this—could you help me?"	"Could you please help me with this?
Noncritical of others	"Why can't you be polite?"	"Please don't use that word to describe me."

To be authentically yourself when you are advocating for what you need, consider the personal qualities you want to express. Some helpful personal qualities that might support your success are listed below. You may like to refer to the list of *Personal Qualities Many People Value* in chapter 7 for more ideas.

Approachable	Focused	Practical
Authentic	Friendly	Proactive
Bold	Generous	Respectful
Collaborative	Grateful	Safe
Competent	Nonjudgmental	Stable
Courageous	Open	Structured
Curious	Optimistic	Thorough
Determined	Passionate	Thoughtful
Fair	Persistent	Understanding

List up to six personal qualities you will aim to convey in your self-advocacy conversations.

_____   _____

_____   _____

_____   _____

Assertive communication seeks to avoid shaming, threatening, confronting, embarrassing, blaming, criticizing, or attacking a person's character, any of which will make the other person defensive and more resistant to change. Being open and respectful increases the chance that your message will be accepted (Lonczak 2020; Pipaş and Jaradat 2010). To influence others, it can be helpful to avoid being overtly emotional and, as much as you can, project calm, rational objectivity, even if you feel very strongly about the issue (Cook and Purkis 2022).

This is the frustrating reality of the double-empathy problem: constantly adapting your communication so that others can understand you. If you are advocating for yourself with a non-neurodivergent person or in an environment that values a neuronormative style of communication (most workplaces), you may be more successful if you replicate some aspects of neuronormative politeness while still expressing the personal qualities that are important to you. This may feel a little like masking, but in this case the goal is to assert yourself in a manner that is most likely to be heard and accepted by others, rather than hide who you are. Performing this kind of assertiveness while staying authentic to who you are could include:

- Staying calm and not fully revealing the intense emotions that underlie your request

- Staying on track and focused on solving the problem

- Speaking with confidence and clarity using a tone of voice that conveys your deep knowledge of the issue

- Carefully listening to the other person's perspective to find common ground and shared values

- Considering a range of solutions, as long as these meet your needs

- Considering the other person's needs and how any suggested changes might affect them

Find a time to have the conversation that suits you and the other person. When they feel relaxed, they will have time to consider your suggestions. The performative nature of this will likely be exhausting for you, so practice self-soothing strategies before and after the conversation, no matter the outcome.

Your Assertive Communication Plan

Consider a change you'd like to make that you can only achieve by asking someone to help you. You can plan your conversation by completing the following table. You'll find a blank version of this worksheet at https://www.newharbinger.com/53073.

Questions	Example Situation	Your Situation
Person's name	Fred	
Relationship to you	Manager	
Concise summary of the problem	Our office is very noisy and disruptive.	
Impact of the problem on you	It takes a lot of energy to concentrate. I am getting headaches and am beginning to get anxious about coming to work.	

Questions	Example Situation	Your Situation
Clear statement of your needs	*I need a quiet workspace.*	
Your rights relevant to this situation	*This reasonable accommodation would make the workplace safe and healthy for me.*	
Your proposed solution: (Assertive statement that describes the outcome you want and is respectful, direct, nonthreatening, noncritical, and non-blaming)	*I would like to work from home two days a week and have access to a quiet room to work in the office. This would help me meet my deadlines without causing exhaustion and anxiety.*	
Personal qualities you want to embody in the conversation	*Competent, fair, nonjudgmental, respectful*	
Uncomfortable emotions that might show up in this conversation	*I am terrified that he will deny my request and I will be stuck working this way or need to find another job.*	
Urge to avoid the uncomfortable emotions	*I want to avoid the whole conversation.*	
How you can self-soothe while still having the conversation	*I can stim before the meeting and remember to breathe. I can acknowledge how hard this is and how much courage it takes to ask for this.*	
Helpful support available to you	*I can ask a colleague to attend the meeting, or I could debrief with them afterward.*	

Briefly describe any emotions and sensations that you noticed when having this conversation.

Emotion: _____ Physical sensation: _____

Emotion: _____ Physical sensation: _____

Emotion: _____ Physical sensation: _____

Make a note of how the other person responded, and outline your next advocacy steps.

_____

_____

_____

You can further prepare yourself for this conversation by saying key statements aloud using a calm, steady, and rational tone of voice. You may also benefit from considering the resistance you may encounter and planning how you would respond to this.

Identify Resistance and Respond with Confidence

Not all your self-advocacy efforts will be successful the first time. However, it can help to remember that when people are reluctant to agree to your requests, it may not be for personal reasons. There are many reasons why people tend to avoid change that emerge from unconscious cognitive biases and have nothing to do with you. These reasons include the following:

1. When people feel out of control in their lives, they try to create certainty wherever they can. Your suggested change may unintentionally undermine their fragile sense of control.

2. People tend to prefer existing systems because they are assumed to be better than any proposed alternative (*status quo bias*).

3. Most people dislike uncertainty. How things are now may not be ideal, but it is familiar. By contrast, change feels uncomfortable or awkward and has an unknown outcome.

4. People tend to resist change if they feel they may lose something even if they also stand to gain from the change (*loss aversion bias*).

5. If the person's safety or security depends on obeying people higher in the social or company hierarchy, they will be more likely to conform to existing rules.

Some of these reasons people are reluctant to consider change might seem nonsensical to you, particularly if, like many neurodivergent people, being consistent with your values is more important to you than fitting into social rules or deferring to authority (Vance 2021). However, these are real, hidden hurdles people must overcome to accept change. Fortunately, you can use this knowledge to inform your approach, gently allay their concerns about potential losses, reinforce the benefits of change, and assure them that others will accept the change too.

Beyond general reluctance to change, you may also encounter different forms of resistance. Passive resistance places the burden on you to keep chasing your goal. By doing nothing, the other person is betting on you giving up. To overcome passive resistance, make sure you are direct and specific in your request, ask when the change will start, and agree to follow up. Stonewalling is a form of resistance that creates obstacles for you to overcome, such as claiming that your request is against company policy when these policies should support people at work, not limit them.

You may be made to feel guilty about affecting others' comfort or needs, putting pressure on you to abandon your request. Your request might be countered with something you have to give in return, such as agreeing to change your work hours only if you will no longer take breaks, or letting you work in a quieter office only if you do extra administrative work. When others demand secrecy regarding your accommodations, it prevents you from accessing additional support and denies others the right to access similar accommodations. Other red flags include outright denial, minimizing the difficulties you face, and veiled threats that pressure you into withdrawing your request.

Below you will find suggestions about how to respond to dismissive or evasive comments confidently and straightforwardly. Some of these could be difficult for you to say, so work within your limits and consider asking someone to support you during the conversation. If someone is making veiled threats or responding in a hostile manner, you are unlikely to reach a resolution and it may be best to walk away from the conversation. Someone with these attitudes is unlikely to ever be supportive.

Potential Obstacles	Confident, Assertive, Straightforward Responses
Guilt and evasion: "We can't give you special treatment." "It wouldn't be fair." "If we do this for you, everyone will want it."	"Everyone has different strengths and challenges. This is about leveling the playing field. The changes I am asking for will make it easier for me to perform at my best. If other people need these changes, they should be able to access them too."

Potential Obstacles	Confident, Assertive, Straightforward Responses
Passive resistance: *Saying "Yes" but not following through.*	Create accountability by following up: "*Let's schedule a meeting in a few weeks to review the changes*" and "*When can I expect to hear back from you?*"
Stonewalling: *"That's not our policy."* *"This is the way we've always done things here."*	"*Yes, I understand. When this policy was written, we didn't know as much about individual differences. We need to change this policy to include people like me who don't fit this expectation.*"
Guilt and obligation: *"Making this change would be too costly."* *"This would be too big a burden."* *"Everyone else is fine with it."*	Hold the person accountable: "*I'm not sure that others would see my wellbeing as a burden, but I am happy to collaborate with the team to find a solution.*"
Demanding secrecy: *"We'd appreciate it if you didn't share this arrangement with others."*	"*Could you explain why I need to keep this a secret? I don't think my silence should be a condition of accessing reasonable accommodations.*"
The support is conditional: *"We'll make this adjustment if you make a change too."*	"*The change I'm asking for would make it easier for me to perform in my role. What you are suggesting could undermine this.*"
Minimizing and patronizing: *"We don't think this will help you."*	"*I am happy to consider any alternative suggestions that would meet this need.*"
Denial and dismissal: *"This is just an excuse."*	"*I am not asking to make my work easier; I am asking for changes that will help me do my work without causing me other problems.*"
Veiled threats: *"Sure, we can make these changes for you. When is your contract being renewed?"*	It may be best to walk away, but you could say, "*I suggest we try the change for a few weeks and see how it goes. If my performance is still meeting expectations, under the law there is no reason my employment should be at risk.*"

Describe a situation where you met resistance in one of the abovementioned ways. Outline the type of resistance and how you responded at the time.

Describe how you would like to respond if this happened again.

Asking for help a second time and supplying extra information allows people to overcome their initial reluctance to change. How they respond will also reveal whether they have any intention of approving your request at all. In some situations, standing up for yourself assertively might result in others seeing you as the problem. In this case, the best solution may be to leave.

Know When to Cut Your Losses

Advocacy is about focusing on what you can change. Despite all your efforts, sometimes you can do nothing to make a situation more comfortable for you. Sometimes people will not listen or help you. Sometimes the job or environment is not a good fit. For example, if you have sensory sensitivities to noise, bright lighting, and conflict, jobs in retail or hospitality are likely to be exhausting. If your workplace is stressful or nonaffirming, continually causes you to burn out, and your efforts for self-advocacy are unsuccessful, you may need to look for other work if you can.

We hope that you can find a place where you can thrive as a neurodivergent person. This may involve leaving behind toxic workplaces, unhealthy environments, or people who don't accept and respect you. An ideal, neurodiversity-affirming workplace is one where:

The focus of the work suits you:

- It aligns with your values—you are doing something you feel is important.

- It is in (or related to) an area of interest.

- Your strengths and abilities are harnessed and appreciated.

All forms of diversity are respected:

- You are treated with dignity and respect.

- Neuronormative expectations are challenged.

- Neurodivergent people are consulted in the design of services that affect them ("nothing about us without us").

- Everyone makes an equal effort to understand each other.

- Facilities are provided that meet the needs of all disabilities and differences.

You are given support to perform at your best:

- Your needs are heard and accommodated.

- Sensory or social stressors are addressed.

- Expectations are clearly stated.

- You are given equal access to services and opportunities.

- Stress is minimized or eliminated.

- You can be yourself and do not need to mask.

- You have control over your workload and timelines.

Consider how affirming and supportive your current workplace or study environment is for you. Describe how you could advocate to make it better or whether you need to be cutting your losses and walking away.

_____

_____

_____

_____

_____

Move Toward What Matters

There is no shame in asking for what you need. It may only take minor adjustments to help you perform at your best and avoid meltdowns, shutdowns, sensory overload, and burnout. However, to achieve this it helps to be clear on what you want to change, and set goals that define small, achievable changes.

Define Your Valued Goals

Setting goals is the process of working out how you'd like things to be better and what you need to do to get there. As discussed in chapter 2, many neurodivergent people set overly ambitious goals based on neuronormative ideals. These are exhausting and difficult to achieve, and therefore more likely to fail (Kemp 2021). If you've struggled to achieve your goals, you may be reluctant to set new ones in case you don't succeed again. To avoid the self-criticism and emotional pain that comes with failure, you might even feel like giving up on your goals.

For much of my adult life, I've experienced some kind of muscular or joint pain. My physical therapist has encouraged me to do exercises and stretches to alleviate this, but it just never became a habit. Eventually, I gave up. Recently, I finally found a way that seemed to work better for my brain. I started by looking for YouTube videos on stretching that showed me different techniques to try. The novelty helped me get started, but what's supported me to keep going is finding that it reduces my pain. I feel better and more in control. I still don't do these stretches every day, but my motivation continues to grow. —Jennifer

You will increase your chance of success if you set goals in ways that make them easier to achieve and motivating for you to complete. Goals are most helpful when they:

1. Are based on your values, not what other people think you should do

2. Are positively phrased and focused on what you want to do, not what you want to get away from

3. Are achievable and a small step in the right direction, rather than too big, vague, or overwhelming

4. Make your life better, consisting of compassionate actions that will improve your experience of life in noticeable ways

5. Allow for continual improvement, understanding that your skills, knowledge, or the frequency of the habit will increase over time

Below, you will find examples of goals that are difficult to achieve and more likely to fail because they only describe what you don't want (negatively phrased), are vague, or demand flawless performance. We've matched these with alternatives that are positively phrased, small and clearly defined, and much more achievable.

Unhelpful Goals	More Helpful Goals
Stop feeling so exhausted	Use an app to remind me to go to bed earlier Take breaks regularly during the day
Stop wasting time	Pursue my creative projects for an hour each week Ask a friend to body double to get my jobs done
Make friends	Get to know the members of my role-playing group better Join a club in my area of interest
Stop people taking advantage of me	Set boundaries with an unsupportive person Say no to unreasonable requests at work
Stop procrastinating	Attend all my lectures this semester Do a weekly "tidy up sprint" in my living room
Stop being late	Set automatic reminders on my phone calendar to get ready 30 minutes before I need to leave

Now it's your turn. Think of a broad goal you'd like to achieve, then rewrite it as several small goals that are positively phrased, aligned with your values, readily achievable, and will make your life better.

Your Broad Goal	Small, Achievable, Value-Based Goals

It's time to pull together what you've learned and use this to create a self-compassionate action plan that defines something important you want to achieve in your life and describes small, achievable steps you can take to get there.

Your Self-Compassionate Action Plan

To complete this activity, start by defining your overall objective and then set up to three achievable, positively phrased goals aligned with your values. For each goal, identify up to three small actions you could take to achieve that goal. Below is an example of a completed plan. You can download a blank version of this worksheet at https://www.newharbinger.com/53073.

Sample Self-Compassionate Action Plan

Overall Objective: *To recover from burnout and have more enjoyable activities in my week*		
Goals	**Values**	**Small Actions**
To spend time with people in ways that don't drain me.	*Connecting with others*	*Tell my friends that I need quiet environments to avoid burnout.*
		Organize a movie night at home.
		Play my new game online with a friend.
Have more energy in the evenings and on weekends for fun activities.	*Connecting with others* *Fun/play*	*Ask my manager if I can work from home 1–2 days per week.*
		Take time to stim after I get home.
		Hire a cleaner once a week.
Spend time on my creative projects.	*Learning* *Creativity* *Fun/play*	*Clear some space for my hobbies.*
		Get out my old, beloved craft projects to tinker with them.
		Research some fun project ideas online.

Now, it's your turn to define your goals by completing the table below. Remember to include a maximum of three small action steps for each goal. Aim to make each action as achievable as possible to get yourself off to a good start and build motivation early on. To identify your values, refer to the themes you identified in chapter 7. (If you haven't completed that activity yet, do it now.)

Overall Objective:		
Goals	**Values**	**Small Actions**

Living a Lifetime of Gentle Returns

One of the originators of ACT, Kelly Wilson, said that we are all living a lifetime of "gentle returns." This means that in any given moment, it is very easy get pulled off track and do things that don't align with your values. The challenge we all face is getting back on track. Living your life according to your values therefore requires consistent effort. By creating goals aligned with what is important to you and assertively communicating your needs, you can create a pathway to a fulfilling and meaningful life for you. Along the way, things may not happen as you expect, and not everyone will be equally helpful. You may get pulled in directions quite different to what you intended. However, persistently making "gentle returns" back to what is important to you will allow you to transform your life in positive ways.

Making a Difference for Yourself and Others

Visions are worth fighting for. Why spend your life making someone else's dreams?

—Tim Burton

Our society is poorer without diversity; we need different perspectives to thrive. With a unique perspective that comes from having different social expectations, neurodivergent people tend to challenge the social hierarchy, call out injustice, and advocate for positive change. We also challenge conventions, speak out when systems are broken, and identify creative solutions to complex problems. However, while we are often lauded for our radical thinking, we are simultaneously shamed for not following established social rules. We should be safe to be ourselves but instead we need to hide who we are. While others may reap the benefits of neurodivergent thinking, the extra challenges we face remain unacknowledged. The personal costs of living in a society that is designed for the majority are rarely considered, yet the negative impact on our physical health, mental health, education, and employment can be profound.

You did not choose to be a member of the neurodivergent community; you were born into it. The challenges you face are not your fault—yet only you can address them. Even if others do not accept you, you can learn to accept yourself. You are an imperfect human simply doing your best. This book was written to meet you in this place and has one broad objective: *to help you understand your neurotype and empower you to create a satisfying and meaningful life that aligns with what is important to you, accommodates your neurodivergent needs, and supports your mental and physical health.* In each chapter, you've been learning how to approach yourself with warmth and openness and judge yourself less harshly. You've begun to orient your life to your values and develop safe relationships with neurokin who share your interests. You are gradually discovering who you are underneath your mask.

This process will evolve over time and at some point will touch every aspect of your life. By working *with* your neurodivergence, capitalizing on your strengths, and allowing compassion to flow from you to yourself, you can build a life that supports and accommodates your difficulties; one in which you also feel more comfortable to ask for what you need. You'll need persistence and courage to make these changes, as well as time and practice—lots of practice. This work will be uncomfortable at times, but it offers the potential for greater joy, satisfaction, and fulfillment.

Fortunately, treating yourself with greater kindness communicates an attitude of acceptance that is contagious. Being unapologetically yourself and allowing others to see you *exactly as you are* empowers others to do the same. If you choose to reveal your neurodivergence, visibly stim, or talk in depth about your interests, you give permission for others to be themselves too. You become a role model for your friends, family, children, and the broader community. By accepting who you are and allowing yourself to *be seen,* you make an important contribution to the broader social justice movement too.

Becoming part of the wider neurodivergent community offers the potential to access unwavering support and a deep sense of belonging. Finding accepting and compassionate spaces to share your experiences will be hugely beneficial to your mental health. Seek out communities where you can give and receive practical support, information, resources, tips, and advice on how to navigate discrimination. You might even join forces to advocate for your rights. Above all, the neurodivergent community offers a chance to celebrate your uniqueness and find humor in everyday challenges.

Before we leave you, we have just one more piece of advice. As you stride out into the world and seek to change things for the better, make sure to conserve enough spoons for your own wellbeing. Choose your battles; you are not responsible for fixing everything that's broken. We need non-neurodivergent people to understand and address these systemic issues, but take care of yourself too. Advocating and educating others will cost more emotional labor than you expect, so remember to make time to self-compassionately rest and recharge. Ahead of you, there is a purposeful and meaningful life. This may take some time to achieve, but your persistence will be worth it. We can't wait to see what you can achieve and wish you success, satisfaction, and joy on your journey from here.

Acknowledgments

Travis: thank you for everything you've done to support me and for picking up everything I've dropped during this process. It's been quite a journey, and I couldn't have done it without you standing behind me, quietly and steadfastly supporting everything I do. Tesilya and the team at New Harbinger: my deepest thanks for your guidance and wise counsel. A big thanks to the wonderful neurodivergent professionals I've been so fortunate to get to know. I've never felt so seen and accepted in my professional life, and thank you for coming to the rescue when I couldn't find the references I needed! Finally, I must acknowledge all my incredible clients, past and present. I deeply appreciate the time we spend together. You teach me something new every day, and are so patient with me as we navigate the world of neurodivergence together. I hope this book offers you some answers.

—Warmly, Jennifer

I would like to acknowledge the support of my AuDHD husband Michael who cooked me meals and gave me space and time to dedicate to writing and many humorous moments: thank you for letting me be me. Thank you to my mother Kim for helping me with practical things over the past year so I could put all my spoons into projects like this book. Thank you to Dr. Michelle Livock, my partner on The Neurodivergent Woman Podcast; my clinical registrar supervisor Gaby Hill, who first introduced me to compassion focused therapy and encouraged me to live by my values; and my boss and mentor Dr. Debbie Jeffries at Redlands Psychologists, who provided me with my first affirming information about Autism and ADHD, has been so supportive, and provided an accommodating workplace. A big thank you to my wonderful clients—I have learned so much walking side by side with you all on your journey—and to the amazing neurodivergent clinician community: we support and uplift one another and talk endlessly about our spins. Being part of this neurodivergent community has felt like coming home.

—Monique

References

American Psychiatric Association (APA). 2022. *Diagnostic and Statistical Manual of Mental Disorders: DSM-5-TR*. 5th edition, text revision. Washington, DC: APA.

Arnold, S. R. C., J. M. Higgins, J. Weise, A. Desai, E. Pellicano, and J. N. Trollor. 2023. "Confirming the Nature of Autistic Burnout." *Autism* 27(7): 1906–1918.

Artemisia. 2018. "Identity: A Beautiful Work in Progress." In *Spectrum Women: Walking to the Beat of Autism*, edited by B. Cook and M. Garnett. London: Jessica Kingsley Publishers.

Askham, A. V. 2020. "Brain Structure Changes in Autism, Explained." *Spectrum News*, October 15. https://www.spectrum news.org/news/brain-structure-changes-in-autism-explained.

Au-Yeung, S. K., L. Bradley, A. E. Robertson, R. Shaw, S. Baron-Cohen, and S. Cassidy. 2019. "Experience of Mental Health Diagnosis and Perceived Misdiagnosis in Autistic, Possibly Autistic and Non-Autistic Adults." *Autism* 23(6): 1508–1518.

Ayers-Glassey, S., and P. D. MacIntyre. 2021. "Investigating Emotion Dysregulation and the Perseveration- and Flow-Like Characteristics of ADHD Hyperfocus in Canadian Undergraduate Students." *Psychology of Consciousness*.

Babinski, D. E., A. Kujawa, E. M. Kessel, K. B. Arfer, and D. N. Klein. 2019. "Sensitivity to Peer Feedback in Young Adolescents with Symptoms of ADHD: Examination of Neurophysiological and Self-Report Measures." *Journal of Abnormal Child Psychology* 47(4): 605–617.

Ball, B., and M. E. J. Newman. 2013. "Friendship Networks and Social Status." *Network Science* 1(1): 16–30.

Bargiela, S., R. Steward, and W. Mandy. 2016. "The Experiences of Late-Diagnosed Women with Autism Spectrum Conditions: An Investigation of the Female Autism Phenotype." *Journal of Autism and Developmental Disorders* 46(10): 3281–3294.

Barkley, R. A. 2020. *Executive Functions: What They Are, How They Work, and Why They Evolved*. New York: Guilford Press.

Barnea-Goraly, N., T. W. Frazier, L. Piacenza, N. J. Minshew, M. S. Keshavan, A. L. Reiss, and A. Y. Hardan. 2014. "A Preliminary Longitudinal Volumetric MRI Study of Amygdala and Hippocampal Volumes in Autism." *Progress in Neuro-Psychopharmacology & Biological Psychiatry* 48: 124–128.

Beaton, D. M., F. Sirois, and E. Milne. 2020. "Self-Compassion and Perceived Criticism in Adults with Attention Deficit Hyperactivity Disorder (ADHD)." *Mindfulness* 11(11): 2506–2518.

———. 2022. "The Role of Self-Compassion in the Mental Health of Adults with ADHD." *Journal of Clinical Psychology* 78(12): 2497–2512.

Bedrossian, L. 2021. "Understand and Address Complexities of Rejection Sensitive Dysphoria in Students with ADHD." *Disability Compliance for Higher Education* 26(10): 4.

Belcher, H. L., S. Morein-Zamir, W. Mandy, and R. M. Ford. 2022. "Camouflaging Intent, First Impressions, and Age of ASC Diagnosis in Autistic Men and Women." *Journal of Autism and Developmental Disorders* 52(8): 3413–3426.

Belek, B. 2019. "Articulating Sensory Sensitivity: From Bodies with Autism to Autistic Bodies." *Medical Anthropology* 38(1): 30–43.

Best, J. R., and P. H. Miller. 2010. "A Developmental Perspective on Executive Function." *Child Development* 81(6): 1641–1660.

Black, M. H., P. J. F. Clarke, E. Deane, D. Smith, G. Wiltshire, E. Yates, W. B. Lawson, and N. T. M. Chen. 2023. "'That Impending Dread Sort of Feeling': Experiences of Social Interaction from the Perspectives of Autistic Adults." *Research in Autism Spectrum Disorders* 101: 1–13.

Bonnello, C. 2022. "The Autistic Not Weird Autism Survey." Accessed July 2023. http://autisticnotweird.com/autismsurvey /?fbclid=IwAR3jiAHJUY1FJ8pjvWkWTSBS54afrp82gusB0IEgRJqwY4zlbQJuUUHngX8.

Boone, M. S., J. Gregg, and L. W. Coyne. 2020. *Stop Avoiding Stuff: 25 Microskills to Face Your Fears and Do It Anyway*. Oakland: New Harbinger Publications.

Botha, M., B. Dibb, and D. M. Frost. 2022. "'It's Being a Part of a Grand Tradition, a Grand Counter-Culture Which Involves Communities': A Qualitative Investigation of Autistic Community Connectedness." *Autism: The International Journal of Research and Practice* 26(8): 2151–2164.

Bottema-Beutel, K., S. K. Kapp, J. N. Lester, N. J. Sasson, and B. N. Hand. 2021. "Avoiding Ableist Language: Suggestions for Autism Researchers." *Autism in Adulthood* 3(1): 18–29.

Bottema-Beutel, K., S. K. Kapp, N. Sasson, M. A. Gernsbacher, H. Natri, and M. Botha. 2023. "Anti-Ableism and Scientific Accuracy in Autism Research: A False Dichotomy." *Frontiers in Psychiatry* 14.

Brown, B. 2015. *The Gifts of Imperfection*. Center City, MN: Hazelden Publishing.

Buckle, K. L., K. Leadbitter, E. Poliakoff, and E. Gowen. 2021. "'No Way Out Except from External Intervention': First-Hand Accounts of Autistic Inertia." *Frontiers in Psychology* 12: 1–17.

Cage, E., and Z. Troxell-Whitman. 2019. "Understanding the Reasons, Contexts and Costs of Camouflaging for Autistic Adults." *Journal of Autism and Developmental Disorders* 49(5): 1899–1911.

Cai, R. Y., and L. Brown. 2021. "Cultivating Self-Compassion to Improve Mental Health in Autistic Adults." *Autism in Adulthood* 3(3): 230–237.

Cai, R. Y., V. Gibbs, A. Love, A. Robinson, L. Fung, and L. Brown. 2023. "'Self-Compassion Changed My Life': The Self-Compassion Experiences of Autistic and Non-Autistic Adults and Its Relationship with Mental Health and Psychological Wellbeing." *Journal of Autism and Developmental Disorders* 53(3): 1066–1081.

Campbell, M. 2018. "Finding Your Tribe." In *Spectrum Women: Walking to the Beat of Autism*, edited by B. Cook and M. Garnett. London: Jessica Kingsley Publishers.

Careaga, M., J. Van de Water, and P. Ashwood. 2010. "Immune Dysfunction in Autism: A Pathway to Treatment." *Neurotherapeutics* 7(3): 283–292.

Casanova, E. L., C. Baeza-Velasco, C. B. Buchanan, and M. F. Casanova. 2020. "The Relationship Between Autism and Ehlers-Danlos Syndromes/Hypermobility Spectrum Disorders." *Journal of Personalized Medicine* 10(4): 260.

Cassidy, S., L. Bradley, R. Shaw, and S. Baron-Cohen. 2018. "Risk Markers for Suicidality in Autistic Adults." *Molecular Autism* 9(1): 42–42.

Cassidy, S., P. Hannant, T. Tavassoli, C. Allison, P. Smith, and S. Baron-Cohen. 2016. "Dyspraxia and Autistic Traits in Adults with and Without Autism Spectrum Conditions." *Molecular Autism* 7(1): 48.

Cassidy, S. A., K. Gould, E. Townsend, M. Pelton, A. E. Robertson, and J. Rodgers. 2020. "Is Camouflaging Autistic Traits Associated with Suicidal Thoughts and Behaviours? Expanding the Interpersonal Psychological Theory of Suicide in an Undergraduate Student Sample." *Journal of Autism and Developmental Disorders* 50(10): 3638–3648.

Cazalis, F., E. Reyes, S. Leduc, and D. Gourion. 2022. "Evidence That Nine Autistic Women out of Ten Have Been Victims of Sexual Violence." *Frontiers in Behavioral Neuroscience* 16: 1–20.

Cerutti, R., A. Zuffianò, and V. Spensieri. 2018. "The Role of Difficulty in Identifying and Describing Feelings in Non-Suicidal Self-Injury Behavior (NSSI): Associations with Perceived Attachment Quality, Stressful Life Events, and Suicidal Ideation." *Frontiers in Psychology* 9: 1–9.

Chan, D. V., J. D. Doran, and O. D. Galobardi. 2023. "Beyond Friendship: The Spectrum of Social Participation of Autistic Adults." *Journal of Autism and Developmental Disorders* 53(1): 424–437.

Charlton, R. A., T. Entecott, E. Belova, and G. Nwaordu. 2021. "'It Feels Like Holding Back Something You Need to Say': Autistic and Non-Autistic Adults Accounts of Sensory Experiences and Stimming." *Research in Autism Spectrum Disorders* 89: 1–11.

Clark, M. L. E., Z. Vinen, J. Barbaro, and C. Dissanayake. 2018. "School Age Outcomes of Children Diagnosed Early and Later with Autism Spectrum Disorder." *Journal of Autism and Developmental Disorders* 48(1): 92–102.

Cook, B., and Y. Purkis. 2022. *The Autism and Neurodiversity Self-Advocacy Handbook: Developing the Skills to Determine Your Own Future*. London: Jessica Kingsley Publishers.

Cooper, K., A. J. Russell, J. Lei, and L. G. E. Smith. 2023. "The Impact of a Positive Autism Identity and Autistic Community Solidarity on Social Anxiety and Mental Health in Autistic Young People." *Autism* 27(3): 848–857.

Cooper, R., K. Cooper, A. J. Russell, and L. G. E. Smith. 2021. "'I'm Proud to Be a Little Bit Different': The Effects of Autistic Individuals' Perceptions of Autism and Autism Social Identity on Their Collective Self-Esteem." *Journal of Autism and Developmental Disorders* 51(2): 704–714.

Cope, R., and A. Remington. 2022. "The Strengths and Abilities of Autistic People in the Workplace." *Autism in Adulthood* 4(1): 22–31.

Courchesne, V., V. Langlois, P. Gregoire, A. St-Denis, L. Bouvet, A. Ostrolenk, and L. Mottron. 2020. "Interests and Strengths in Autism, Useful but Misunderstood: A Pragmatic Case-Study." *Frontiers in Psychology* 11: 1–13.

Crenshaw, K. 1991. "Mapping the Margins: Intersectionality, Identity Politics, and Violence Against Women of Color." *Stanford Law Review* 43(6): 1241–1299.

Croen, L. A., O. Zerbo, Y. Qian, M. L. Massolo, S. Rich, S. Sidney, and C. Kripke. 2015. "The Health Status of Adults on the Autism Spectrum." *Autism* 19(7): 814–823.

Crompton, C. J., S. Hallett, D. Ropar, E. Flynn, and S. Fletcher-Watson. 2020. "'I Never Realised Everybody Felt as Happy as I Do When I Am Around Autistic People': A Thematic Analysis of Autistic Adults' Relationships with Autistic and Neurotypical Friends and Family." *Autism* 24(6): 1438–1448.

Crompton, C. J., D. Ropar, C. V. M. Evans-Williams, E. G. Flynn, and S. Fletcher-Watson. 2020. "Autistic Peer-to-Peer Information Transfer Is Highly Effective." *Autism* 24(7): 1704–1712.

Crompton, C. J., M. Sharp, H. Axbey, S. Fletcher-Watson, E. G. Flynn, and D. Ropar. 2020. "Neurotype-Matching, but Not Being Autistic, Influences Self and Observer Ratings of Interpersonal Rapport." *Frontiers in Psychology* 11: 1–12.

Crompton, R. J., and C. Bond. 2022. "The Experience of Transitioning to Adulthood for Young People on the Autistic Spectrum in the UK: A Framework Synthesis of Current Evidence Using an Ecosystemic Model." *Journal of Research in Special Educational Needs* 22(4): 309–322.

Csecs, J. L. L., V. Iodice, C. L. Rae, A. Brooke, R. Simmons, L. Quadt, et al. 2022. "Joint Hypermobility Links Neurodivergence to Dysautonomia and Pain." *Frontiers in Psychiatry* 12: 1–13.

Davis, K. C. 2022. *How to Keep House While Drowning: A Gentle Approach to Cleaning and Organising.* London: Penguin Random House.

den Houting, J. 2019. "Neurodiversity: An Insider's Perspective." *Autism* 23(2): 271–273.

Dwyer, P. 2022. "The Neurodiversity Approach(Es): What Are They and What Do They Mean for Researchers?" *Human Development* 66(2): 73–92.

Edey, R., J. Cook, R. Brewer, M. H. Johnson, G. Bird, and C. Press. 2016. "Interaction Takes Two: Typical Adults Exhibit Mind-Blindness Towards Those with Autism Spectrum Disorder." *Journal of Abnormal Psychology* 125(7): 879–885.

Egan, V., O. Linenberg, and E. O'Nions. 2019. "The Measurement of Adult Pathological Demand Avoidance Traits." *Journal of Autism and Developmental Disorders* 49: 481–494.

Evans, J. A., E. J. Krumrei-Mancuso, and S. V. Rouse. 2023. "What You Are Hiding Could Be Hurting You: Autistic Masking in Relation to Mental Health, Interpersonal Trauma, Authenticity, and Self-Esteem." *Autism in Adulthood* 1–12.

Faraone, S. V., and H. Larsson. 2019. "Genetics of Attention Deficit Hyperactivity Disorder." *Molecular Psychiatry* 24(4): 562–575.

Farmer, G. M., J. L. Ohan, A. L. Finlay-Jones, and D. M. Bayliss. 2023. "Well-Being and Distress in University Students with ADHD Traits: The Mediating Roles of Self-Compassion and Emotion Regulation Difficulties." *Mindfulness* 14(2): 448–459.

Fiene, L., M. J. Ireland, and C. Brownlow. 2018. "The Interoception Sensory Questionnaire (ISQ): A Scale to Measure Interoceptive Challenges in Adults." *Journal of Autism and Developmental Disorders* 48(10): 3354–3366.

Flentje, A., N. C. Heck, J. M. Brennan, and I. H. Meyer. 2020. "The Relationship Between Minority Stress and Biological Outcomes: A Systematic Review." *Journal of Behavioral Medicine* 43(5): 673–694.

Forde, J., P. M. Bonilla, A. Mannion, R. Coyne, R. Haverty, and G. Leader. 2022. "Health Status of Adults with Autism Spectrum Disorder." *Review Journal of Autism and Developmental Disorders* 9(3): 427–437.

Forward, S., and D. Frazier. 2019. *Emotional Blackmail: When the People in Your Life Use Fear, Obligation, and Guilt to Manipulate You*. New York: HarperCollins.

Friedman, C. 2023. "Ableism, Racism, and the Quality of Life of Black, Indigenous, People of Colour with Intellectual and Developmental Disabilities." *Journal of Applied Research in Intellectual Disabilities* 36(3): 604–614.

Galvin, J., A. Howes, B. McCarthy, and G. Richards. 2021. "Self-Compassion as a Mediator of the Association Between Autistic Traits and Depressive/Anxious Symptomatology." *Autism* 25(2): 502–515.

George, R., and M. A. Stokes. 2018. "Gender Identity and Sexual Orientation in Autism Spectrum Disorder." *Autism* 22(8): 970–982.

Gilbert, P. 2009. *The Compassionate Mind*. London: Constable.

Grant, S., S. Norton, R. F. Weiland, A. M. Scheeren, S. Begeer, and R. A. Hoekstra. 2022. "Autism and Chronic Ill Health: An Observational Study of Symptoms and Diagnoses of Central Sensitivity Syndromes in Autistic Adults." *Molecular Autism* 13(1): 1–16.

Groen, Y., U. Priegnitz, A. B. M. Fuermaier, L. Tucha, O. Tucha, S. Aschenbrenner, M. Weisbrod, and M. Garcia Pimenta. 2020. "Testing the Relation Between ADHD and Hyperfocus Experiences." *Research in Developmental Disabilities* 107: 1–11.

Hayden, C. 2022. *Different, Not Less: A Neurodivergent's Guide to Embracing Your True Self and Finding Your Happily Ever After*. Sydney: Murdoch Books.

Hayes, S. C., K. D. Strosahl, and K. G. Wilson. 2016. *Acceptance and Commitment Therapy: The Process and Practice of Mindful Change*. 2nd ed. New York: Guilford Press.

Hedley, D., and M. Uljarević. 2018. "Systematic Review of Suicide in Autism Spectrum Disorder: Current Trends and Implications." *Current Developmental Disorders Reports* 5(1): 65–76.

Henderson, D., S. Wayland, and J. White. 2023. *Is This Autism? A Guide for Clinicians and Everyone Else*. New York: Routledge.

Hess, P. 2022. "Pathological Demand Avoidance in Autism, Explained." *Spectrum Autism Research News*, August 11. https://www.spectrumnews.org/news/pathological-demand-avoidance-in-autism-explained.

Higgins, J. M., S. R. C. Arnold, J. Weise, E. Pellicano, and J. N. Trollor. 2021. "Defining Autistic Burnout Through Experts by Lived Experience: Grounded Delphi Method Investigating #AutisticBurnout." *Autism* 25(8): 2356–2369.

Houghton, D. C., J. R. Alexander, C. C. Bauer, and D. W. Woods. 2018. "Abnormal Perceptual Sensitivity in Body-Focused Repetitive Behaviors." *Comprehensive Psychiatry* 82: 45–52.

Hull, L., L. Levy, M.-C. Lai, K. V. Petrides, S. Baron-Cohen, C. Allison, P. Smith, and W. Mandy. 2021. "Is Social Camouflaging Associated with Anxiety and Depression in Autistic Adults?" *Molecular Autism* 12(1): 1–13.

Hull, L., K. V. Petrides, C. Allison, P. Smith, S. Baron-Cohen, M.-C. Lai, and W. Mandy. 2017. "'Putting on My Best Normal': Social Camouflaging in Adults with Autism Spectrum Conditions." *Journal of Autism and Developmental Disorders* 47(8): 2519–2534.

Instanes, J. T., A. Halmøy, A. Engeland, J. Haavik, K. Furu, and K. Klungsøyr. 2017. "Attention-Deficit/Hyperactivity Disorder in Offspring of Mothers with Inflammatory and Immune System Diseases." *Biological Psychiatry* 81(5): 452–459.

Iversen, S., and A. N. Kildahl. 2022. "Case Report: Mechanisms in Misdiagnosis of Autism as Borderline Personality Disorder." *Frontiers in Psychology* 13: 1–6.

Kamath, M. S., C. R. Dahm, J. R. Tucker, C. L. Huang-Pollock, N. M. Etter, and K. A. Neely. 2020. "Sensory Profiles in Adults with and Without ADHD." *Research in Developmental Disabilities* 104: 1–7.

Kanfiszer, L., F. Davies, and S. Collins. 2017. "'I Was Just So Different': The Experiences of Women Diagnosed with an Autism Spectrum Disorder in Adulthood in Relation to Gender and Social Relationships." *Autism* 21(6): 661–669.

Kanner, L. 1943. "Autistic Disturbances of Affective Contact." *Nervous Child* 2: 217–250.

Kapp, S. K., R. Steward, L. Crane, D. Elliott, C. Elphick, E. Pellicano, and G. Russell. 2019. "'People Should Be Allowed to Do What They Like': Autistic Adults' Views and Experiences of Stimming." *Autism* 23(7): 1782–1792.

Karaca, S., A. Saleh, F. Canan, and M. N. Potenza. 2017. "Comorbidity Between Behavioral Addictions and Attention Deficit/Hyperactivity Disorder: A Systematic Review." *International Journal of Mental Health and Addiction* 15(3): 701–724.

Keezer, R. D., S. I. Leib, L. M. Scimeca, J. T. Smith, L. R. Holbrook, D. W. Sharp, K. J. Jennette, G. P. Ovsiew, Z. J. Resch, and J. R. Soble. 2021. "Masking Effect of High IQ on the Rey Auditory Verbal Learning Test in an Adult Sample with Attention Deficit/Hyperactivity Disorder." *Applied Neuropsychology: Adult* 1–9.

Kemp, J. 2021. *The ACT Workbook for Perfectionism: Build Your Best (Imperfect) Life Using Powerful Acceptance and Commitment Therapy and Self-Compassion Skills*. Oakland: New Harbinger Publications.

Kervin, R., C. Berger, S. J. Moon, H. Hill, D. Park, and J. W. Kim. 2021. "Behavioral Addiction and Autism Spectrum Disorder: A Systematic Review." *Research in Developmental Disabilities* 117: 1–9.

Kidwell, K. E., R. L. Clancy, and G. G. Fisher. 2023. "The Devil You Know Versus the Devil You Don't: Disclosure Versus Masking in the Workplace." *Industrial and Organizational Psychology* 16(1): 55–60.

Kirby, J. N. 2017. "Compassion Interventions: The Programmes, the Evidence, and Implications for Research and Practice." *Psychology and Psychotherapy* 90(3): 432–455.

Kirby, J. N., C. L. Tellegen, and S. R. Steindl. 2017. "A Meta-Analysis of Compassion-Based Interventions: Current State of Knowledge and Future Directions." *Behavior Therapy* 48(6): 778–792.

Knott, R., B. Johnson, J. Tiego, O. Mellahn, A. Finlay, K. Kallady, J. K. Buitelaar, and M. A. Bellgrove. 2021. "The Monash Autism-ADHD Genetics and Neurodevelopment (MAGNET) Project Design and Methodologies: A Dimensional Approach to Understanding Neurobiological and Genetic Aetiology." *Molecular Autism* 12(1): 1–55.

Kolts, R. 2016. *CFT Made Simple: A Clinician's Guide to Practicing Compassion-Focused Therapy*. Oakland: New Harbinger Publications.

La Buissonnière-Ariza, V., J. Alvaro, M. Cavitt, B. M. Rudy, S. L. Cepeda, S. C. Schneider, E. McIngvale, W. K. Goodman, and E. A. Storch. 2021. "Body-Focused Repetitive Behaviors in Youth with Mental Health Conditions: A Preliminary Study on Their Prevalence and Clinical Correlates." *International Journal of Mental Health* 50(1): 33–52.

Lai, M.-C., M. V. Lombardo, A. N. V. Ruigrok, B. Chakrabarti, B. Auyeung, P. Szatmari, F. Happé, and S. Baron-Cohen. 2017. "Quantifying and Exploring Camouflaging in Men and Women with Autism." *Autism* 21(6): 690–702.

Leedham, A., A. R. Thompson, R. Smith, and M. Freeth. 2020. "'I Was Exhausted Trying to Figure It Out': The Experiences of Females Receiving an Autism Diagnosis in Middle to Late Adulthood." *Autism* 24(1): 135–146.

Leonard, S. R. K., and C. Willig. 2021. "The Experience of Living with Very High Empathy: A Critical Realist, Pragmatic Approach to Exploring Objective and Subjective Layers of the Phenomenon." *Counselling and Psychotherapy Research* 21(1): 52–65.

Lilley, R., W. Lawson, G. Hall, J. Mahony, H. Clapham, M. Heyworth, S. R. C. Arnold, J. N. Trollor, M. Yudell, and E. Pellicano. 2022. "'A Way to Be Me': Autobiographical Reflections of Autistic Adults Diagnosed in Mid-to-Late Adulthood." *Autism* 26(6): 1395–1408.

Lindsay, S., K. Fuentes, V. Tomas, and S. Hsu. 2023. "Ableism and Workplace Discrimination Among Youth and Young Adults with Disabilities: A Systematic Review." *Journal of Occupational Rehabilitation* 33(1): 20–36.

Livingston, L. A., P. Shah, V. Milner, and F. Happé. 2020. "Quantifying Compensatory Strategies in Adults with and Without Diagnosed Autism." *Molecular Autism* 11(1): 1–10.

Lonczak, H. S. 2020. "What Is Assertive Communication? 10 Real-Life Examples." *Positive Psychology*, September 3. https://positivepsychology.com/assertive-communication.

Maddox, B. B., and S. W. White. 2015. "Comorbid Social Anxiety Disorder in Adults with Autism Spectrum Disorder." *Journal of Autism and Developmental Disorders* 45(12): 3949–3960.

Maenner, M. J., Z. Warren, A. R. Williams, E. Amoakohene, A. V. Bakian, D. A. Bilder, et al. 2023. "Prevalence and Characteristics of Autism Spectrum Disorder Among Children Aged 8 Years—Autism and Developmental Disabilities Monitoring Network, 11 Sites, United States, 2020." *MMWR Surveillance Summaries* 72(No. SS-2): 1–14.

Mantzalas, J., A. L. Richdale, A. Adikari, J. Lowe, and C. Dissanayake. 2022. "What Is Autistic Burnout? A Thematic Analysis of Posts on Two Online Platforms." *Autism in Adulthood* 4(1): 52–65.

Maroney, M. R., and S. G. Horne. 2022. "'Tuned Into a Different Channel': Autistic Transgender Adults' Experiences of Intersectional Stigma." *Journal of Counseling Psychology* 69(6): 761–774.

Martini, M. I., R. Kuja-Halkola, A. Butwicka, E. Du Rietz, B. M. D'Onofrio, F. Happé, et al. 2022. "Sex Differences in Mental Health Problems and Psychiatric Hospitalization in Autistic Young Adults." *JAMA Psychiatry* 79(12): 1188–1198.

McGeoch, P. D., and R. Rouw. 2020. "How Everyday Sounds Can Trigger Strong Emotions: ASMR, Misophonia and the Feeling of Wellbeing." *BioEssays* 42(12): 1–10.

Milioni, A. L. V., T. M. Chaim, M. Cavallet, N. M. de Oliveira, M. Annes, B. dos Santos, et al. 2017. "High IQ May 'Mask' the Diagnosis of ADHD By Compensating for Deficits in Executive Functions in Treatment-Naïve Adults with ADHD." *Journal of Attention Disorders* 21(6): 455–464.

Miller, D., J. Rees, and A. Pearson. 2021. "'Masking Is Life': Experiences of Masking in Autistic and Nonautistic Adults." *Autism in Adulthood* 3(4): 330–338.

Miserandino, C. 2003. "The Spoon Theory." But You Don't Look Sick (blog). https://butyoudontlooksick.com/articles/written-by-christine/the-spoon-theory.

Monk, R., A. J. O. Whitehouse, and H. Waddington. 2022. "The Use of Language in Autism Research." *Trends in Neurosciences* 45(11): 791–793.

Murray, D., M. Lesser, and W. Lawson. 2005. "Attention, Monotropism and the Diagnostic Criteria for Autism." *Autism* 9(2): 139–156.

Myles, B. S., M. L. Trautman, and R. L. Schelvan. 2013. *The Hidden Curriculum for Understanding Unstated Rules in Social Situations for Adolescents and Young Adults.* Shawnee Mission, KS: Autism Asperger Publishing Co.

Nadal, K. L. 2019. "A Decade of Microaggression Research and LGBTQ Communities: An Introduction to the Special Issue." *Journal of Homosexuality* 66(10): 1309–1316.

O'Nions, E., F. Happé, E. Viding, and I. Noens. 2021. "Extreme Demand Avoidance in Children with Autism Spectrum Disorder: Refinement of a Caregiver-Report Measure." *Advances in Neurodevelopmental Disorders* 5(3): 269–281.

Oredipe, T., B. Kofner, A. Riccio, E. Cage, J. Vincent, S. K. Kapp, P. Dwyer, and K. Gillespie-Lynch. 2023. "Does Learning You Are Autistic at a Younger Age Lead to Better Adult Outcomes? A Participatory Exploration of the Perspectives of Autistic University Students." *Autism* 27(1): 200–212.

Owens, A. P., C. J. Mathias, and V. Iodice. 2021. "Autonomic Dysfunction in Autism Spectrum Disorder." *Frontiers in Integrative Neuroscience* 15: 1–10.

Parenteau, C. I., L. A. Lampinen, S. S. Ghods, J. L. Taylor, R. E. Adams, S. L. Bishop, and S. Zheng. 2023. "Self-Reported Everyday Sources of Happiness and Unhappiness in Autistic Adults." *Journal of Autism and Developmental Disorders* 1–11.

Peleikis, D. E., M. Fredriksen, and S. V. Faraone. 2022. "Childhood Trauma in Adults with ADHD Is Associated with Comorbid Anxiety Disorders and Functional Impairment." *Nordic Journal of Psychiatry* 76(4): 272–279.

Perry, E., W. Mandy, L. Hull, and E. Cage. 2022. "Understanding Camouflaging as a Response to Autism-Related Stigma: A Social Identity Theory Approach." *Journal of Autism and Developmental Disorders* 52(2): 800–810.

Phung, J., M. Penner, C. Pirlot, and C. Welch. 2021. "What I Wish You Knew: Insights on Burnout, Inertia, Meltdown, and Shutdown from Autistic Youth." *Frontiers in Psychology* 12: 1–14.

Pierce, C. 1970. "Offensive Mechanisms." In *The Black Seventies*, edited by F. B. Barbour, 265–282. Boston: Porter Sargent.

Pipaş, M. D., and M. Jaradat. 2010. "Assertive Communication Skills." *Annales Universitatis Apulensis: Series Oeconomica* 2(12): 649–656.

Preece, D. A., R. Becerra, A. Allan, K. Robinson, W. Chen, P. Hasking, and J. J. Gross. 2020. "Assessing Alexithymia: Psychometric Properties of the Perth Alexithymia Questionnaire and 20-Item Toronto Alexithymia Scale in United States Adults." *Personality and Individual Differences* 166: 1–8.

Price, C. J., and C. Hooven. 2018. "Interoceptive Awareness Skills for Emotion Regulation: Theory and Approach of Mindful Awareness in Body-Oriented Therapy (MABT)." *Frontiers in Psychology* 9(May): 1–12.

Price, D. 2021. *Laziness Does Not Exist: A Defense of the Exhausted, Exploited, and Overworked.* New York: Atria Books.

———. 2022. *Unmasking Autism: The Power of Embracing Our Hidden Neurodiversity.* London: Monoray.

Radulski, E. M. 2022. "Conceptualising Autistic Masking, Camouflaging, and Neurotypical Privilege: Towards a Minority Group Model of Neurodiversity." *Human Development* 66(2): 113–127.

Raymaker, D. M., A. R. Teo, N. A. Steckler, B. Lentz, M. Scharer, A. Delos Santos, S. K. Kapp, M. Hunter, A. Joyce, and C. Nicolaidis. 2020. "'Having All of Your Internal Resources Exhausted Beyond Measure and Being Left with No Clean-Up Crew': Defining Autistic Burnout." *Autism in Adulthood* 2(2): 132–143.

Reuben, K. E., C. M. Stanzione, and J. L. Singleton. 2021. "Interpersonal Trauma and Posttraumatic Stress in Autistic Adults." *Autism in Adulthood* 3(3): 247–256.

Riquelme, I., S. M. Hatem, and P. Montoya. 2016. "Abnormal Pressure Pain, Touch Sensitivity, Proprioception, and Manual Dexterity in Children with Autism Spectrum Disorders." *Neural Plasticity* 2016: Article 1723401.

Rommelse, N., M. van der Kruijs, J. Damhuis, I. Hoek, S. Smeets, K. M. Antshel, L. Hoogeveen, and S. V. Faraone. 2016. "An Evidenced-Based Perspective on the Validity of Attention-Deficit/Hyperactivity Disorder in the Context of High Intelligence." *Neuroscience and Biobehavioral Reviews* 71: 21–47.

Rommelse, N. N. J., B. Franke, H. M. Geurts, C. A. Hartman, and J. K. Buitelaar. 2010. "Shared Heritability of Attention-Deficit/Hyperactivity Disorder and Autism Spectrum Disorder." *European Child and Adolescent Psychiatry* 19(3): 281–295.

Rosenberg, E. L., and P. Ekman. 1995. "Conceptual and Methodological Issues in the Judgment of Facial Expressions of Emotion." *Motivation and Emotion* 19(2): 111–138.

Rumball, F., L. Brook, F. Happé, and A. Karl. 2021. "Heightened Risk of Posttraumatic Stress Disorder in Adults with Autism Spectrum Disorder: The Role of Cumulative Trauma and Memory Deficits." *Research in Developmental Disabilities* 110: 1–14.

Rumball, F., F. Happé, and N. Grey. 2020. "Experience of Trauma and PTSD Symptoms in Autistic Adults: Risk of PTSD Development Following DSM-5 and Non-DSM-5 Traumatic Life Events." *Autism Research* 13(12): 2122–2132.

Russell, G., S. K. Kapp, D. Elliott, C. Elphick, R. Gwernan-Jones, and C. Owens. 2019. "Mapping the Autistic Advantage from the Accounts of Adults Diagnosed with Autism: A Qualitative Study." *Autism in Adulthood* 1(2): 124–133.

Sandin, S., P. Lichtenstein, R. Kuja-Halkola, C. Hultman, H. Larsson, and A. Reichenberg. 2017. "The Heritability of Autism Spectrum Disorder." *JAMA* 318(12): 1182–1184.

Sandoz, E., and T. DuFrene. 2013. *Living with Your Body and Other Things You Hate: How to Let Go of Your Struggle with Body Image Using Acceptance and Commitment Therapy.* Oakland: New Harbinger Publications.

Sasson, N. J., D. J. Faso, J. Nugent, S. Lovell, D. P. Kennedy, and R. B. Grossman. 2017. "Neurotypical Peers Are Less Willing to Interact with Those with Autism Based on Thin Slice Judgments." *Scientific Reports* 7(1): 1–10.

Schippers, L. M., L. I. Horstman, H. van der Velde, R. R. Pereira, J. R. Zinkstok, J. C. Mostert, C. U. Greven, and M. Hoogman. 2022. "A Qualitative and Quantitative Study of Self-Reported Positive Characteristics of Individuals with ADHD." *Frontiers in Psychiatry* 13: 1–14.

Sciberras, E., J. Streatfeild, T. Ceccato, L. Pezzullo, J. G. Scott, C. M. Middeldorp, P. Hutchins, R. Paterson, M. A. Bellgrove, and D. Coghill. 2022. "Social and Economic Costs of Attention-Deficit/Hyperactivity Disorder Across the Lifespan." *Journal of Attention Disorders* 26(1): 72–87.

Shakes, P., and A. Cashin. 2020. "An Analysis of Twitter Discourse Regarding Identifying Language for People on the Autism Spectrum." *Issues in Mental Health Nursing* 41(3): 221–228.

Sheppard, E., D. Pillai, G. T.-L. Wong, D. Ropar, and P. Mitchell. 2016. "How Easy Is It to Read the Minds of People with Autism Spectrum Disorder?" *Journal of Autism and Developmental Disorders* 46(4): 1247–1254.

Sosnowy, C., C. Silverman, P. Shattuck, and T. Garfield. 2019. "Setbacks and Successes: How Young Adults on the Autism Spectrum Seek Friendship." *Autism in Adulthood* 1(1): 44–51.

Steindl, S. R. 2020. *The Gifts of Compassion: How to Understand and Overcome Suffering.* Samford Valley, AU: Australian Academic Press.

Stoddard, J. A., and N. Afari. 2014. *The Big Book of ACT Metaphors: A Practitioner's Guide to Experiential Exercises and Metaphors in Acceptance and Commitment Therapy.* Oakland: New Harbinger Publications.

Strang, J. F., L. Kenworthy, A. Dominska, J. Sokoloff, L. E. Kenealy, M. Berl, et al. 2014. "Increased Gender Variance in Autism Spectrum Disorders and Attention Deficit Hyperactivity Disorder." *Archives of Sexual Behavior* 43(8): 1525–1533.

Sundberg, M. 2018. "Online Gaming, Loneliness and Friendships Among Adolescents and Adults with ASD." *Computers in Human Behavior* 79: 105–110.

Syharat, C. M., A. Hain, A. E. Zaghi, R. Gabriel, and C. G. P. Berdanier. 2023. "Experiences of Neurodivergent Students in Graduate STEM Programs." *Frontiers in Psychology* 14: 1–16.

Tan, C. D. 2018. "'I'm a Normal Autistic Person, Not an Abnormal Neurotypical': Autism Spectrum Disorder Diagnosis as Biographical Illumination." *Social Science and Medicine* 197: 161–167.

Tint, A., H. K. Brown, S. Chen, M.-C. Lai, L. A. Tarasoff, S. N. Vigod, S. Parish, S. M. Havercamp, and Y. Lunsky. 2021. "Health Characteristics of Reproductive-Aged Autistic Women in Ontario: A Population-Based, Cross-Sectional Study." *Autism* 25(4): 1114–1124.

Twohig, M. P., M. E. Levin, and C. W. Ong. 2021. *ACT in Steps: A Transdiagnostic Manual for Learning Acceptance and Commitment Therapy.* New York: Oxford University Press.

van Rensburg, R., H. P. Meyer, S. A. Hitchcock, and C. E. Schuler. 2018. "Screening for Adult ADHD in Patients with Fibromyalgia Syndrome." *Pain Medicine* 19(9): 1825–1831.

Vance, T. 2021. "The Identity Theory of Autism: How Autistic Identity Is Experienced Differently." *Neuroclastic*, October 17. https://neuroclastic.com/the-identity-theory-of-autism-how-autistic-identity-is-experienced-differently.

Volkow, N. D., G.-J. Wang, S. H. Kollins, T. L. Wigal, J. H. Newcorn, F. Telang, et al. 2009. "Evaluating Dopamine Reward Pathway in ADHD." *JAMA* 302(10): 1084.

Waizbard-Bartov, E., E. Ferrer, B. Heath, D. S. Andrews, S. Rogers, C. M. Kerns, C. Wu Nordahl, M. Solomon, and D. G. Amaral. 2023. "Changes in the Severity of Autism Symptom Domains Are Related to Mental Health Challenges During Middle Childhood." *Autism* 0(0): 1–15.

Weir, E., C. Allison, and S. Baron-Cohen. 2022. "Autistic Adults Have Poorer Quality Healthcare and Worse Health Based on Self-Report Data." *Molecular Autism* 13(1): 1–19.

Welch, C., D. Cameron, M. Fitch, and H. Polatajko. 2021. "Living in Autistic Bodies: Bloggers Discuss Movement Control and Arousal Regulation." *Disability and Rehabilitation* 43(22): 3159–3167.

Williams, M. 2004. *The Velveteen Rabbit.* London: Egmont Books.

Williams, M. T. 2020. "Microaggressions: Clarification, Evidence, and Impact." *Perspectives on Psychological Science* 15(1): 3–26.

Willoughby, D., and M. A. Evans. 2019. "Self-Processes of Acceptance, Compassion, and Regulation of Learning in University Students with Learning Disabilities and/or ADHD." *Learning Disabilities Research and Practice* 34(4): 175–184.

Wilson, K., and T. Dufrene. 2010. *Things Might Go Terribly, Horribly Wrong: A Guide to Life Liberated from Anxiety.* Oakland: New Harbinger Publications.

Wilson, R. B., A. R. Thompson, G. Rowse, R. Smith, A.-S. Dugdale, and M. Freeth. 2023. "Autistic Women's Experiences of Self-Compassion After Receiving Their Diagnosis in Adulthood." *Autism* 27(5): 1336–1347.

Wise, S. J. 2022. *The Neurodivergent Friendly Workbook of DBT Skills.* Sydney, AU: Lived Experience Educator.

World Health Organization (WHO). 2019. "International Statistical Classification of Diseases and Related Health Problems, 11th Revision." WHO. https://icd.who.int.

Jennifer Kemp, MPsych, is a privately practicing clinical psychologist based in Adelaide, South Australia, who works with neurodivergent adults experiencing perfectionism, eating disorders, obsessive-compulsive disorder (OCD), and chronic illness. Using a neurodiversity-affirming approach, Jennifer weaves together acceptance and commitment therapy (ACT), and behavioral and compassion-focused approaches with her own lived experience as a late-diagnosed Autistic ADHDer, to help her clients improve their mental health and develop greater self-compassion, self-acceptance, and pride in their neurodivergent identity. Jennifer juggles clinical practice with writing, presenting, and clinical supervision. She is author of *The ACT Workbook for Perfectionism*.

Monique Mitchelson, MPsych, is an Autistic and ADHD clinical psychologist working in private practice in Brisbane, Australia. She is cohost of *The Neurodivergent Woman Podcast*, balancing this with private clients, consultations, training, advocacy, and advising on policy. Monique has a particular interest in the intersection between trauma, chronic illness/pain, and neurodivergence, and works therapeutically with neurodivergent adults using ACT, mindfulness, compassion-focused approaches, and eye movement desensitization and reprocessing (EMDR).

Foreword writer **Sonny Jane Wise** is a neurodivergent, trans, and disabled public speaker, as well as a disability advocate as @livedexperienceeducator. They are cochair for the Australian National Autism Strategy's Social Inclusion Working Group, and author of two books: *The Neurodivergent Friendly Workbook of DBT Skills* and *We're All Neurodiverse*.

MORE BOOKS from
NEW HARBINGER PUBLICATIONS

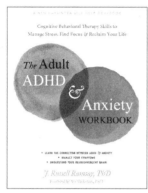

**THE ADULT ADHD AND
ANXIETY WORKBOOK**

Cognitive Behavioral Therapy Skills
to Manage Stress, Find Focus,
and Reclaim Your Life

978-1648482434 / US $25.95

**A RADICAL GUIDE FOR
WOMEN WITH ADHD**

Embrace Neurodiversity,
Live Boldly, and Break
Through Barriers

978-1684032617 / US $21.95

**DBT SKILLS FOR HIGHLY
SENSITIVE PEOPLE**

Make Emotional Sensitivity
Your Superpower Using
Dialectical Behavior Therapy

978-1648481055 / US $18.95

CBT FOR SOCIAL ANXIETY

Simple Skills for Overcoming Fear
and Enjoying People

978-1648481208 / US $19.95

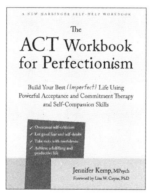

**THE ACT WORKBOOK
FOR PERFECTIONISM**

Build Your Best (Imperfect) Life
Using Powerful Acceptance and
Commitment Therapy and
Self-Compassion Skills

978-1684038077 / US $24.95

**THE BETTER BOUNDARIES
GUIDED JOURNAL**

A Safe Space to Reflect on Your
Needs and Work Toward Healthy,
Respectful Relationships

978-1648482755 / US $19.95

newharbingerpublications

1-800-748-6273 / newharbinger.com

(VISA, MC, AMEX / prices subject to change without notice)

Follow Us 📷 ❓ 𝕏 ▶ 📌 in ♪ ⑥

Don't miss out on new books from New Harbinger.
Subscribe to our email list at **newharbinger.com/subscribe** 🖱

Did you know there are **free tools** you can download for this book?

Free tools are things like **worksheets, guided meditation exercises**, and **more** that will help you get the most out of your book.

You can download free tools for this book—whether you bought or borrowed it, in any format, from any source—from the New Harbinger website. All you need is a NewHarbinger.com account. Just use the URL provided in this book to view the free tools that are available for it. Then, click on the "download" button for the free tool you want, and follow the prompts that appear to log in to your NewHarbinger.com account and download the material.

You can also save the free tools for this book to your **Free Tools Library** so you can access them again anytime, just by logging in to your account! Just look for this button on the book's free tools page.

+ Save this to my free tools library

If you need help accessing or downloading free tools, visit **newharbinger.com/faq** or contact us at **customerservice@newharbinger.com.**